T0195560

Potpourri
of Life

Sandra L Reynolds - Webster

authorHOUSE®

AuthorHouse™
1663 Liberty Drive
Bloomington, IN 47403
www.authorhouse.com
Phone: 1 (800) 839-8640

Published by AuthorHouse 02/26/2020

ISBN: 978-1-7283-4822-3 (sc)
ISBN: 978-1-7283-4821-6 (e)

Library of Congress Control Number: 2020903952

Print information available on the last page.

Scripture taken from The Holy Bible, King James Version. Public Domain

Introduction

I have written this compilation of verse hoping to encourage and inspire others to live with hope and full of joy. I have said "see you later" to two husbands and two children and wonder at His mercy. I'm still here full of strength and determination. Many experiences in my life and the lives of family and friends can be gleaned from these pages, from childhoods to this present day. I'm trusting that you too will remember the similar events from yesteryears with laughter and perhaps some tears. Give Him praise and thanksgiving for the battles fought and won. He's faithful and will never leave you alone. He's the God of love…He loves us…you and me. Amen

Yours in love,
Sandra R. Webster

Acknowledgement

I have written this compilation of verse hoping to encourage and inspire others to live with hope and full of joy. I have said "see you later" to two husbands and two children and wonder at His mercy. I'm still here full of strength and determination. Many experiences in my life and the lives of family and friends can be gleaned from these pages, from childhoods to this present day. I'm trusting that you too will remember the similar events from yester years with laughter and perhaps some tears. Giving Him praise and thanksgiving for the battles fought and won. He's faithful and will never leave you alone. He's the God of love…He loves us, you and me.

I want to take this time to thank my daughters (Renee, Sherrise, Loretta, Lisa, Nolleen and Lauren), for their prayers support and encouragement through the years. I am complete novelist when it comes to technology (computer workings) How, when and why they function as they do, so a special thanks goes to "Nol" for helping in the technical processes required for publication by the publishers. I'm sure she was often frustrated in my lack of understanding, yet in and through her love for me, she patiently so the manuscript to completion. Thanking the Lord for her abilities and perseverance.

—Sandra R. Webster

I Know I'm Free,

Bondage no Longer in my Vocabulary

This I know down deep in my soul
No matter by my head, what I am told
I will prosper as the Word proclaims
if I keep on trusting in Jesus' precious name.

The Word I know, by faith, is true
God the Father loves me and He loves you
In due time He sent Jesus to be our guide
My sins have been forgiven, I don't have to hide.

Christ's blood makes me guiltless in God's eyes
Jesus paid my debt in full when
on the cross He died
False guilt is senseless, I no longer it endure
My debt's been paid at Calvary,
of this I am quite sure.

So in worship I acknowledge,
The Love that set me free
I've been washed in His blood,
Jesus lives for you and me
There was no other way to pay the debt I owe
So to Calvary He went, so His love I would know.

Contents

Introduction v
Acknowledgement vii
I Know I'm Free, ...ix

CHAPTER I
Living Through Life

Choose Life 1
We too must be Industrious 2
Things Will Change 3
Sea of Life 4
If You're Smart 5
To Parents 6
Shut Your Mouth 7
In My Solitude 8
In This Life 9
He Loves Me No More 10
In Sweet Memory 12
Flowers for His Teacher 13
A Sinner's Confession 14
Prepare 15
Dark and Luscious 16
I'm only Human 17
Bread Winner Under Pressure 18
Broke but Not Broken 19

Let Jesus Handle It 20
Victimized/Now Physically Free 21
One of Life's Maturing Experiences...............................22
A Manic Depressive 23
The Demon of Hatred 24
Woe Is Me! 25
Be Happy, They Grow up 26
Traveling in the Spirit 27
Saved..28
Release and Relief...29
I'm A Winner..30
Confession 31
Caterpillar to Butterfly 32
Search Yourself..33
Self-pity 35
So You are Ninety-one Years Young 36

CHAPTER II
The Triune God: Father Son Holy Ghost

He's Faithful..39
Jesus, Our Peace with God..40
Jesus, Promise Keeper 41
Love is Lord 42
Jesus Loves Me 43
His Majesty is Compassionate 45
He is Trustworthy..46
Have You Claimed Him as Lord....................................47
I feel my Father's Love 48
Security a Surety...49
I'm Saved..50
God, Our Father Loves Us...51
Saviour and Lord...53

Walking on the Water 54
Jehovah-Jireh 56
What a Friend 57
Only Dust Apart From His Spirit 58
It's Not Yours 59
What does God See? 60
When You are Called To Serve 61
Determined Love 62
No Longer the Same 63
Do Everything in Him 64
The Lord is Faithful 66

CHAPTER III
Just a Verse or Two

Choose Ye This Day 69
Be Ready 71
Beginning Again 72
Broken Hearted 73
Bits of Wisdom 74
Advice 75
Spring 76
Truth 77
I'm Listening 78
Rendered Praise 79
Room for Solitude 80
Salvation 81
Praise Him 82
O Sailor 83
Move On 84
Love 85
Look Up 86
I Depend on You, Lord 87

I'm Sure 88

I Belong to God 89

Seek And Ye Shall Find 90

The Love of God 91

Welcome, New Born 92

Work of Art 93

Frustration Cries 94

Thank You Lord 95

Saints! 96

Here's another Truth 97

Deliverer 98

Thanks 99

Never Forget 100

CHAPTER IV
Encourages / Encouragement

Be Thou Encouraged 103

Press On 104

Keep Trusting Him 105

Nourish Your Faith 106

Obedience is better than Sacrifice 107

Anticipation 108

Let's Live His Love 109

"Vengeance is Mine" 110

We Must Fight to Win the Prize 111

Accept The Challenge 112

Bible Truth 113

By Faith 114

I am so Proud of You 115

What are YOU Doing? 116

His command 118

Listen and Obey 119

An Adage of Old 120
Keep Climbing 121
We Are Set Apart, Sanctified 122
Examine Yourself 123
Nearer My God to Thee 124
I'm Brand New 125
Though l Have Many Idiosyncrasies 126
Ready 128
New Born 129

CHAPTER V
Seasons Seasonal Times

Respect and Freedom Emerging? 133
Easter's Reflection Prayer 135
Our Flag of Representation 136
To Mothers 137
Heavenly Hospitality 138
Thanksgiving Day Prayer 139
Winter's Approaching 141
On Those Blue Days 142
Confident in Recession/Depression 143
Autumn's Windy Arrows 144
Salute to Mothers 145
Celebration 146
The Wearing of White 147
Christ is Christmas 149
Submission for Redemption 150

CHAPTER VI
Greif-Sorrow, Saying Farewell

Sorrow will soon end 153
The Sorrow of Grief 154

There Will be A Reunion Rejoicing 155

Be ready It's Almost that Time 156

We Will Exchange These Earthy Houses 157

Look up, He's Coming! 159

Limited time 160

When all is said and Done 161

Trust Him 162

Epitaph 163

Freedom Everlasting 164

Expectation 165

Sorrow 166

Hope to See You Soon 167

Things Will Change 168

Heavenly Hospitality 169

CHAPTER VII

Today is Tomorrow's Memory

Today is Tomorrow's Memory 173

24 Hours Together 175

A Prayer for Restored Health 176

Be Careful, Be Sure 177

Living is not Easy 178

Betrayed 179

You and I 180

It is The Love of God 181

People, Changed 182

Enduring Loneliness 183

I am not Just a Body 184

Friends? 185

Where Are You? 186

Trust in God 187

Philosophical Observation 188

Complexity of Emotions 189
What We Call 190
At the End of each Day 191
The Best Thing to Do 192

CHAPTER VIII
Prayer – Praise

Through it All 195
Jesus Prayed for Me 196
Remind Me Lord 197
Thank You 198
Praise and Thanksgiving for Eternal Life 199
My Prayer for Malachi 200
I am, Will Be 201
To a Christian Lady I Know 202
Thank You Lord for Mercy and Grace 203
Lest I Forget 204
I Praise Him 205
Thanks So Much 206
Praise 207
Live In Me 208
We Thank God for You 209
A Prayer of Empathy 210
Healing Power 211
Patience Is A Struggle For Me 212
Listening to Me Lord? 213
Prayer 214
This Parent's Prayer Letting Go and Trusting God 215
Because We Belong to You 217
Intercession 218
Christians Sing 219
Good morning Lord 220

Telling it Like it Is... 221
Troubled in my Spirit.. 222
Turn It Over to Jesus... 223
Proverbs for Abundant Living........................... 224
A Christian's Prayer for the Unsaved............... 225
May We Abide 227
What I Must Do?... 228
Telling it Like it Is... 231
Troubled in my Spirit.. 232
Turn It Over to Jesus... 233
Proverbs for Abundant Living........................... 234
A Christian's Prayer for the Unsaved............... 235
May We Abide 236
What I Must Do... 237

Chapter I

Living Through Life

Choose Life

Stress kills
Calm down
Be still some times Play the clown.
Stress destroys Enjoy your life Family matters Elude strife.
Stress kills
Invoke God's peace Meditate
So joy may increase.

We too must be Industrious

Like a gecko holding on
I climb to reach the top
No time to stop.
Like the ant wisely I work
Preparing for tomorrow
My duties I cannot shirk.

Like the coney building on a rock
Small I may be
I come from tenacious stock.
Now, we like the locust
Must band together
To fight against the enemy
In all kinds of weather.

Proverbs 30

Things Will Change

There's nothing like a good hardy laugh
To dismiss those salty tears
As we age in years let's laugh more often
Down here, we've not many more years.
When looking back a tear may fall
Yet there were many, many times
That laughter filled the days gone by
And heart bells from gladness chimed.
Laughter and tears all parts of this life
Pain and suffering we've endured too
But soon in Eternity for the Saints
There'll be radian\joy filled skies of blue.
Look up all you saints of our Sovereign God
And bless his holy eternal, everlasting name
For our God speaks truth and is faithful
He's promised peace and joy from the ashes of shame.

Sea of Life

Swimming in life's waters
Isn't all up stream
Sometimes we float along
And realize some of our dreams.
Then there come those stormy times
When it seems that we will drown
And in spite of the windy tempests
God's gracious mercy abounds.
When our sailing again is smooth
And we think back upon the storms
We can thank the Lord our Saviour
We are learning to trust and conform.

If You're Smart

Satan desires to steal away your soul
God desires to make you whole.
Satan desires to sift you as wheat
The Lord wants you walking on Straight Street.
Now, you choose this day,
just whom you want to serve.
Remember, tomorrow is not promised
and Heaven is not what you deserve.
If you're smart, you'll choose life
And give your heart to the Lord
It's the only way to live
Better hurry and get on board.

To Parents

God gives to us children, to care for
To teach, love and train
That in all He may be glorified
Plant the seeds for His grace and mercy to rain.
God gives children to His saints
As blessings from his hands and his heart
He expects them to be given back for service
As we live and teach them so His love they will impart.

Shut Your Mouth

What seems to be obvious, isn't always as it seems
There can be episodes of reality, nightmares or dreams.
For years one may suppose this or that to be true
Later to discover actuality was nowhere in view.
Some people say it .... and why wouldn't they know?
So others assume that what was said must be so.
Unless you have walked every step of my way
You cannot be certain of what's said
or what another may say.
Have you ever been told something and then you believed?
To later learn it wasn't so from the heart that was grieved.
Sometimes the harm done is in the mind's thoughts
But a soul can be massacred, a heart made distraught.
Many things spoken are bare faced suppositions and lies
Contrived truths, that shock and damage
ignorant (innocent) lives.
Be careful what you say even what
you are tempted to think
Someone's life may be teetering just on the brink.
Advice: Matthew 7: 12

In My Solitude

When fear of tomorrow keeps me awake at night
The Comforter keeps me company
His very presence dissipates the fright.
And in the darkness of my sleepless nights
The spirit is my reminding Light
"Lo I am with you" .... I read
I know His voice and my heart it delights.
In the still and the quiet of any night
That I am restless and cry out for peace
I read in His Word
"peace be still ..." and the fear takes flight.
In the stillness this particular night
As this year moves often violently to its end
And no earthly friends are around me
I ponder my past ways .... which of them should I amend
Which are worthy to defend?

In This Life

After joy, there's sorrow
After laughter, woe and tears
Days turn into weeks
And months roll into years.
In this life we often worry
Will we gain or will we lose
Then we fret about our losses
bitterness is the response we choose.
When we revel in times of happiness
Wake up tomorrow and it's gone
We wonder why such brief respite
We so often feel like pawns.
No matter what we have
Or how much we may attain
Prosperity here isn't always promised
What's more important is to give not gain.
Whether joy or sorrow
Whether laughter, woe or pain
Alive in want or plenty
His way and will his word explains

He Loves Me
No More

Why did you go and leave us here?
Crushed, broken and filled with fear.
Fear for the future and what ii might hold
You took my love, her daddy, and the dreams untold.

Your last words cut and yes my heart they did tear,
Yet my love for you still forces me IO care.
But you go on as though no harm and no foul.
You walk away from your wife and child, how?

Your little girl asks, "What is wrong, is it me?"
And does she still have the love of her Daddy?
I look in those brown eyes and see sadness and fear,
For the loss of her Daddy she loves and hold, dear.

I tell her you love her and you always will, for sure
And that it's only me that Daddy loves no more.
She smiles at first, feeling safe again, hopeful and secure
Then suddenly frowns, seeing my
pain for what 1 must endure.

Endure a life of loneliness without
her daddy, my true love,
It's an emptiness that's mirrored in the gray skies above.
But she knows we Jove her and that will never change
So now ii 's our lives without you, we need to arrange.

Reality forces me to go on ti/ God calls me home,
But it leaves me lonely and wanting to groan,
"Take me soon Father, away from this pain,
Take me home to your kingdom
where eternity's my gain."

There's nothing to keep me here anymore
For the truth of my life is, he loves me no more
Our little girl has all the love from
God and us she will need
So I worry and cry not for the life she might lead.

With your words you have erased all that I hold dear
And those words will always and forever ring in my ear
But please love her more tenderly or else I fear
The way of true love for her will never be clear.

My heart is dead, and I desire that my body should die too,
To die in peace with no more tears
or fears to pierce me through
From you I want no pity, no sorrow, hold your tears
lust make sure our baby girl is loved
for the rest of her years.

When God calls me home across that glorious shore
This time I am ready because you love me no more
So tell our baby always, I love her and wish her happiness.
And for your life, be happy, without me
maybe you 'II find true bliss.

Written 7/29/00 by Teal D. Reynolds-Mouzon

In Sweet Memory

Mother, words cannot express
All the love I feel deep inside
They seem so inadequate to convey
How much my heart is filled with pride.

I know you prayed both night and day
by God's grace, supplied all my needs
I'm proud to say by all your sacrifices
you sowed into me, life's true seed.

You exemplified God's patience
as you loved me in spite of myself
And I will never, ever forget you
for nurturing me in wisdom's wealth.

I'm remembering you in my heart
as in spirit, I behold your face
I believe you are now surrounded
by His light in His Holy Place.
You showed me by your love, The Saviour
As God revealed Himself to you
I'll praise you forever dear Mother
in showing me God's love, l grew.

That you were led by His Holy Spirit
As you taught me in word and deed
So again by God's grace, dear Mother
in His Word I do faithfully feed.

Flowers for His Teacher

A certain teacher planning her day
Was unexpectedly offered wild flowers
from the hands of a bright and eager boy.
His dark and dancing eyes full of pride
Looked at the flowers that were grass laced
though crushed and tiny they unfolded
in his soft, little hand of innocent grace.
Images of innocent love filled her mind before she spoke
"thank you so much" ... "sweetheart"
the intrinsic beauty of his injured offering
She thought them a special, awesome spiritual treat.
Via the hands and heart of a little boy
So like Jesus, lowly, meek and mild
God rendered her again his abiding love
via the sensitive act of a precious child.
While on the street one summer's day
That young boy called her by name
The teacher turned to see her flower child
Smiling as he always did, lovingly the same.
For a retired educator to be remembered
By a child she once cared for and taught
Brings such happiness to the heart
No where could such satisfaction have been bought.

A Sinner's Confession

For many years I kept running
I said the words repeatedly again and again
But I really didn't know Him or evaluate my sin.
I didn't know Jesus then
Though I knew his name and about his fame
But I didn't know him, to my shame.
I didn't know the one I was obeying
Would turn on me one day
Really didn't want to know, sure didn't pray.
So many years in ignorance were wasted
My soul in jeopardy so long
I now desire to know and denounce all my wrongs.
I have repented Lord of all my sins
Teach so I can witness for Thee
I want the world to know, they too can be set free.
Now that I've come to see myself
The scriptures are living and alive
I seek every day to be spiritually revived.
Thank you Lord, my Saviour
Your love and truth has opened my eyes
I'm walking in The Light and now I realize.
No more endless worry filled nights for me
Because of Christ's sacrifice my soul is at peace
My fears of Hell and death have ceased.
That you saved me unto eternal life
In your mercy and grace I'm longing to grow
So that I may witness to others so they may know.

Prepare

Step into the shower of Grace
To cleanse your heart and mind
The Water will never cease
God's mercy is eternal and divine.
Bathe your face in joy and love
Drench your bands in peace
Move your lips in compassion
_the Kingdom of God will increase.
Be a living, vibrant testimony
To His mercy and power to save
He thought God's creation worthy
Jesus submitted and His life He gave.

Dark and Luscious

Chocolate Dark or milk, bitter or sweet
No one really can compete.
In this world of dark and light
Chocolate, what a soothing sight.
Chocolate, dark or light
Rich and warm
There's no denying us
So you better calm that storm.
We're here to stay, aren't going anywhere
So you might as well the facts face and accept
We're the heat that melts your chill
We're not shallow, we've got plenty depth.
Chocolate, dark, light or bright
We too, are God's creation
Therefore being white don't make you right,
we too, are precious in His sight

I'm only Human

There are times when I worry
Times when all I can do is fret
There are times when I'm scared
Times I'm filled with regret.
There are times when I feel lonely
Times when I feel afraid
Times when I feel forsaken
Times when doubt my soul invades.
There are times I'm not happy
times when I feel very sad
But when I meditate on the words of Jesus
Spiritual peace makes my heart glad.
I know that I can't trust my feelings
I can't rely on my family and friends
So when my very soul is needy
On Christ I know I can always depend.

Bread Winner Under Pressure

Sign of the time

LORD, I've got to talk to you
So much stuff is on my mind
Even your folks get on my last nerve
They push the wrong buttons lots of the time.
I'm worried, frustrated and a little depressed
Will you tell me how to pay my bills
Lord, I know it can't all be my fault
And help me out of the stress that kills.
My kids are bugging me with "gimme"
Can I have some money for this and that
My spouse nags me about the trash and garbage
By the way Lord, make her get rid of that cat.
Our money problems can't be my fault
I just don't make enough money to satisfy
I can't ride the bus in my fine business suits
I needed that car we couldn't afford to buy.
Now the preacher says I'm the man of the house
I don't think my family believes it by the way they act
Rolling their eyes and sucking their teeth
I don't get no respect and that's a fact.
I'm stuck in a rut don't know how to get out
Taking another job is out of the question
Nobody believes me when I tell them
"There ain't no more jobs, we're in a depression".

18

Broke but Not Broken

I'm feeling down again
Want to know why?
I'm broke but not broken
Financially I'm bone dry.
I struggle to stay afloat
Pinching pennies as I go
Paying tithes and offerings
I can't hold on to a little dough.
Today, I'm down to a handful of coins
Days before I see any paper money
Most of it already spoken for, in theory spent
If things weren't serious, they would be funny.

Let Jesus Handle It

The lie they told,
let it go and live
Don't harbor pain
Give it over,.. forgive!
The person or persons
who meant you great harm
Know God's got your back
He's your shield, rest in his arms.
He will fight all of your battles
He'll protect and He'll defend
You don't ever, ever have to worry
In Jesus relax, on him depend.
He loves you so much that His angels stand guard
They protect your soul and mind day by day
His Holy Spirit speaks to comfort you within
He relays to God every prayer that you pray.

Victimized / Now Physically Free

From a pretty girl to a burdened young Mom
inexperienced, lead astray out of fear, wrong choices
a father figure once her threatening seducer
she believed others and obeyed the wrong voices.
Used, abused, bewildered and deeply troubled
Intimidated by devious and cruel Godless lovers
She managed with her children to endure all the shame
Ashamed feeling she had no one to shelter her or cover.
held hostage in bondage in strange places
So distant and remote from all those who truly cared
Verbally threatened and no tangible means for her escape
Battered emotionally and physically,
with children, she despaired.
Then Light broke through and her will to live revived
After years of vile treatment and debilitating scorn
She made up her mind to endure degradation no longer
The Holy Spirit spoke get out, "you're
a child of God, reborn"
Courage endowed and power received,
she broke away from her husband
Fear didn't die until his death set her troubled mind at ease
She's learning to live her life seeking
health and understanding
Though visible and invisibly scarred, she
lives via prayer and praise on her knees

One of Life's Maturing Experiences

Teen love so often fickle
They're up and then low down
Those tears shed are briny as pickles
They wear the face of a clown.
They wear their hearts on their sleeves
Blinded by the day's rising sun
Tomorrow in sadness they'll grieve
When they find out they're not the only one.
Hey, did you see him with another girl?
Lips locked like liquid glue
Your anger like a whirlpool swirls
When you realize he's been lying to you.
Don't worry and don't you cry my dear
There's time to meet your soul's mate, never fear
Ask God to give you the mate that's his choice
And when He does, praise Him loud and clear.

A Manic Depressive

At times I feel vacant, in a dark
space ... unreasonably fearful
Cracked ...... Broken ..... leaking or incomplete
With-out defined identity, and in my thoughts
I'm upside down while on my feet
I am over whelmed by the bodies of people I meet.
Sometimes void of the need to speak or greet
I have the urge to sob, to weep, can't sleep
Often sobbing and I don't know why ...
I blame others for my misery and that's why I cry.
I require attention on my terms, getting it until ....
I'm sure they wish I'd take a pill and chill
People get tired and backing off, go their ways
My moods are draining and they don't know what to say.
Why do I surrender to the emotional turmoil of anguish ...
is it for me, more comfortable to surrender than to resist?
Howbeit, by faith and determination, I press on
And one day all my fears and discontent will be gone.

The life a friend of mines once lived

The Demon
of Hatred

Cancerous, is the disease known as hatred
For it shows no mercy in its aggression
It will persist to devour like a cancer
It will destroy the hater if there's not confession.
So be ever vigilant with God's help
To afford it no home in your heart
Reject its intrusion immediately
Or you'll regret ever letting it start.
If you don't, you will pay an awful price
If you daily feed it with intent
You'll not affect the one hated
If your heart willingly receives rent.
Hatred is another tool of the deceiver
This demon is after your soul
It'll dry up your sense to forgive
Making you bitter, lonely and cold.
So in faith be hopeful and trust the Lord
Though the suffering and nausea is real
Pray for courage and divine strength
Let faith and mercy be your heart's reveal.

Woe Is Me!

I don't know why
Some things happen to me When down,
I get stepped on Agony just won't let me be.
When I'm hungry
No food can be found
When I'm thirsty
I'm given coffee grounds.
When I'm shoeless
Tacks are everywhere When I'm naked
Does anyone really care?
When I'm lonely
Not a friend comforts me
When I'm sad and crying
It's because I feel so lonely.

Be Happy,
They Grow up

Your children won't always be childish
They'll grow up, will they smile
when they think of you
Have you lived out your love toward them
Is your faith and trust in God showing through?
Then relax in the promises of God
Cover them in prayer and trust the Lord
He'll guide and they will understand with children
of their own, they'll appreciate what you endured.

Traveling in the Spirit

I rode the bus this morning
As usual the driver greeted me
I found I had a choice of seats
And you sat down with me.
The ride was very pleasant
Your sun was shining bright
I thought such peaceful thoughts
That my spirit breathed in delight.
When it was time to exit
One bus to board the next
It was waiting there for us
My spirit was not vexed.
Riding to my job
I said a silent prayer
And ended it with "Guide me Lord,
I'm in your tender care."
So filled was I with peace
I felt your presence all around
I knew that I could face this day
No matter what "went down."
Arriving at my destination
My hand upon the door's knob
I took a deep breath and entered
prepared by thy Spirit to do my job.

Saved

I'm clothed and ready to fight
I'm dressed up for battle
I'm anchored in the Light
On my head Salvation's helmet
My breastplate is in place
And God's love, I can't forget.
Calloused hands are fit for the plow
My feet are Heaven bound
And no one can stop me now.

Release and Relief

So often it seems my burdens
Are more than I can bear
When weighted down by worries
I wonder does Jesus really care?
But then I remember
If I focus on the problems
Say "why is this happening to me?"
I will hinder the solution
Lord, let me just give them to Thee"
I must give them all to Jesus
On His shoulders let them rest
And I will know true peace of mind
As He relieves me of all stress.

Psalms 55:22
Matthew 11:28, 29
1 Peter 5:7

I'm A Winner

I don't know how and I don't know when
I know victory is ours and all the good guys win.

Satan now is buffeting us day and night
But the Lord is our defender and wins all the fights.

Though I don't know how and I don't know when
I know that we are conquerors as the Lord defends.

So we must hold on while the
winds of adversity blow
Have patience and endure, it's the way faith grows.

Satan may retreat awhile to
regroup for attack again
But no matter his strategy, the war he'll never win.

We will fight many battles before we take our rest
Our Commander in Chief is with
us through each test.

Confession

I must stop striving to be perfect
Learn to rest in the providence of God
He is faithful and will not fail me
He will perfect me as on earth I trod.
I can not be perfected if
I allow not His Spirit to lead
I must humbly accept this fact
Or my progression I will impede.
God knows everything about me
He knows my true heart's desires
So I must learn to endure in patience
As gold, I will be refined in life's fire.
And when I've gone through every trial
Successfully through valleys and over the hills
I will be perfected and at peace
Surrendered, succumbed to His holy Will.
Submissive and still, He will teach me
How to live and work for His glory
I must be at peace in order to teach
and give witness of Salvation's story.

Caterpillar to Butterfly

THE OLD ME IS DEAD, CRUCIFIED,
LONG TIME AGO
I'M A NEW CREATURE IN AND
BECAUSE OF CHRIST
I'VE BEEN REDEEMED BY HIS SHED BLOOD
FOR ME, HE PAID GOD'S AWFUL PRICE.
I'M NEW AND PERFECT IN SPIRIT
I HA VE NOT THE DESIRE WITHIN TO SIN
I'M NOW LIVING AND ALIVE
BECAUSE OF JESUS
BY HIS DEATH AND RESURRECTION, I WIN.
I'VE BEEN SAVED FROM
ETERNAL DAMNATION
BORN AGAIN INTO A BRAND
NEW WAY OF LIFE
WHEN HE RETURNS MY
SALVATION COMPLETED
THANKS TO JESUS THE SON
OF GOD, THE CHRIST.
I'M A LIVING WITNESS, MY
SOUL HAS BEEN SET FREE
I'M A LIVING WITNESS TO HIS
MERCY AND GRACE
I'M SO PROUD TO BE CALLED A CHRISTIAN
THE HOLY SPIRIT GIVES ME COURAGE
TO CONTINUE THE RACE.

Search Yourself

Today, whom did you make happy?
What did you do, what did you say?
Did you sacrifice to Satan?
Or to The Lord did you pray?
Did you think a mean or evil thought?
If so, Satan smiled ear to ear
Or did you pray a prayer of blessing
That made the eyes of angels tear?
Did you sing a song of thanksgiving?
Was His Spirit given control?
Or did you curse someone in anger,
Which child did you unjustly scold?
Did you go to church in humility?
Was your heart full of Zion's songs?
Did you listen to the preacher's message?
Confess your weaknesses and your wrongs?
Were you happy to be among believers?
Or did you go lo confess your sins?
Did you accept The Lord's forgiveness?
Or did you fall for Satan's chagrin?
If you confessed and repented
You received pardon and a fresh start
But if you denied your faults
You left defeated and with a troubled heart.
For Lucifer Devil is a liar
The BOOK says 'fie is the Father of lies
His desire is to separate and destroy you
Jesus came to give you abundant life.

Believe the Word and though life
may not always be kind
You'll be happy with Jesus alone
This old troubled world will lose its attraction
And your Heavenly Father will
guide you safely Home.

Self-pity

Have you ever wanted to backward go?
How to God you've wish it could be so
The changes that we would have made
May have been subtle but would incite a parade.
Can you remember a happy place or state
Perhaps when you were allowed to finally date
Or was it when in the agony of pure ecstasy
Was it a memory of when you
were in love with me?
Right now in your heart is there any hope of joy
Is there any experience you wish to employ?
Do you pray for a place and time in this today,
When your sorrow and troubles
would simply go away?
Have you felt that tears aren't worth crying?
But you could not figure out how to stop
Is there a sick gnawing in your turbulent gut,
Or soulful whimper, like that of a friendless mutt?
I can tell you friend, you're having a really bad day
I know, "cause there have been
times I've felt that way
In fellowship let's get together
and pray our way out
We're too experienced to quit, with
Him we've too much clout.

So You are Ninety-one Years Young

We recognize your many years, Grand-mom
You are, have been by God truly blessed
your loving deeds and steadfast joy
always to your faith continuously attest.
Because of God's grace and mercy
We honor you on this glorious day
For ninety-one years of serving the Lord
We know He's guiding you the rest of the way.
You've offered heart and hands in service
Your many prayers for others ascend to his throne
Your walk has been steadfast, steady and long
Know that we love you too, you're never alone.

Chapter II

The Triune God: Father Son Holy Ghost

He's Faithful

The Lord always keeps his Word
Provides for everyone of my needs
Fills my heart with thanksgiving
My soul he tenderly feeds.

He endows me with hope
Forgave all of my sins
Repentance is all that he asks
To maintain fellowship with him.

His love revitalizes in all ways
His protection means faithful security
He desires trust and obedience
He is our salvation absolutely.

Jesus, Our Peace with God

God's peace will keep you calm
His love will bring joy and comfort
His power will give you confidence
His faithfulness will give you assurance.

The hope of God will always inspire
And his holiness will purify
His forgiveness is the form of cleansing
His grace and mercy cannot be denied.

His strength strengthens and empowers
His Word instructs us in righteousness
His Spirit reminds, leads and guides us
His sovereignty affords us peaceful rest.

His atonement for our sins appeased the Father
His submission to God's will secured our future.
Amen, thank you JESUS

Jesus, Promise Keeper

When suffering seems to reside
in your soul and on every side.

Though anguished, don't submit
His grace is sufficient it never quits.

No truer friend has ever lived
He suffered and died abundant life to give.

He'll be with you in your darkest hours
He'll be your fortress and high tower.

Prayers of praise and thanksgiving do
He's promised and He will, take care of you.

Love is Lord

Lord, you know me inside out
You know what life and death are all about.

You know the results of Salvation and sin
Knowing all you know, you took me in.

Love you know me through and through
Every word, work and thought false and true.

You know my enemies and know my friends
You have been my Saviour, no beginning no end.

You are holy, eternal, sovereign and you are life
You are building your church to be your faithful wife.

And while you are working on growing us up
With joy overflowing dear Lord, fill my cup.

Jesus Loves Me

Jesus loves me
How about that
Me! Jesus really loves me
It's a biblical fact.
Jesus loves me
I'm a child of the King
Jesus loves me
An eternal song I have to sing.
As a child I heard the message
A long, long time ago
God gave me faith to believe
Grace and mercy I now know.
I heard that God desires
To bless and fellowship with man
Because of man's sin, the Father
Made provision by salvation's plan.
This loving God favored a young lady
Her name was Mary, we all know
And she received the Holy Spirit's words
Within her the promised Seed began to grow.
You see ...
The Angels could not redeem man
The animals and fowls are not our kind
So God gave ns Jesus by virgin birth
He saved his children through a royal line.
We only have to Believe ... the truth
Repent receive Him and salvation is so
We will live to enjoy eternity forever
Forgiven. Redeemed, Saints, the Bible tells ns so.

Oh, yes the Father loves me
He loves you too, it's true
Christ's death and resurrection are proof
And there's his empty tomh for all to view.
And now He sits beside his Father
Enthroned; for the saints He intercedes
He's preparing a place for God's family to live
He's coming back for ns on clouds of celestial speed.

His Majesty is Compassionate

There are times when we're bewildered
Times we are troubled and afraid
But our faith should be firm in Jesus
All our concerns on him laid.

He's reigning now in Glory, Saviour He
He sees and knows all things
He'll support us in our endeavors
He's Lord of Lord and King of Kings.

He hears those quiet groanings
He's sensitive to our woe and sorrows
His tender mercies never wane
His compassion is never shallow.

He is Trustworthy

God never makes mistakes
He forgets not one detail
He never abandons His children
He strengthens, so we may prevail.

God has never nor will He ever lie
Never changes His commands
He's always kind and compassionate
We can trust Him to always understand.

God is Sovereign and Holy, He's Just
No power on Earth in Heaven or Hell
Can diminish His glory and wisdom
His Spirit or voice, ever quell.

Have You Claimed Him as Lord

Jesus, He is our Saviour, that we know
Of your life, is He Lord and have you confessed it's so?
Does he get your attention, is He in control
Or do you inform him how and where you want to go?

Do you say Lord, "lead me in all of life's way
I relinquish my will unto you
I will follow you wherever you lead me to go
Keep me Lord faithful and true.
Lead me guide me, I surrender all
Keep me, shield lest I fall
I believe your promises to me are true
Because of grace and mercy I belong to you.

I worship you my God and my King
You are more than life, you are everything
I open to you fully the door of my heart
Lord Jesus, by your love keep me, never to be apart."

I feel my Father's Love

Daddy holds me regally in His arms
And His hugs comfort me tenderly
He sets me back upon my feet
Directs and guides me ever so gently.

Daddy rocks me in His arms at night
And I look expectantly into His eyes
Oh, how they glisten from His tears of love
I know He loves me, I'm His precious prize.

Daddy protects and shields me in all storms
No torrents of wind or water can hinder me
When others in terror and frustration wail
It's a privilege to greet Him on my knees.

Security a Surety

No truer friend has ever lived
No greater love can any give
He's with us in our darkest hours
He's our fortress and high tower.

When suffering seems to reside
In our souls and on every side
Though anguished we must not submit
His grace is sufficient, it never quits.

Praise and thanksgiving we must always do
He's promised to take care of me and you.

Though often we may walk in solitude
Our heavenly Father deserves our gratitude
In joy or sorrow, awake or sleep
God's own angels watch and keep.

I'm Saved

My eyes have been opened
Thank God I now can see
That the road I was traveling
The Lord never meant for me.
My eyes have been opened
My soul's been revived
I'm a new born creation
Now, I'm spiritually alive.
By his grace and mercy I'm enthralled
The Bible told me it would be so
My ears have been opened
For myself, salvation I know.
So, I thank you so much Jesus
For loving the likes of me
I know you to be ever faithful
You are truth, in you I am free.

God, Our Father Loves Us

5/16/08

In this life we seek tangible and intangible things
We exert ourselves striving for this and that
It 's so easy to forget in success or failure, that
God understands and He's always got our backs.

What we want may not be His desire for us just now
In our ascension, setbacks and denials are stepping stones
We must keep on climbing, and stop looking back
Trust in God He knows best and by him we are known.

Some plans for our personal lives, He has yet to reveal
When they unfold, the wonder will
delete the present pains
Don't be disheartened our sight and strength are limited
Stay on the battlefield and fight, the
struggles are not inane.

In every difficulty He encourages us to stay the course
To keep pressing when we just want to give up and die
When we are disappointed, He knows how much we hurt
For He listens to our prayers and sorrowful cries.

We must accept that our Merciful
God, knows what He's doing
Especially when we can't see and do not understand
And remember that His love for us
was costly and is eternal
We are essentially the prime subjects of His Holy plan.

Saviour and Lord

Into this hostile world He came
A bundle endowed with joy
Once wrapped in swaddling clothes
King Jesus came as a baby boy.

Often sought to be destroyed
He grew into a sinless man
He healed the lame and cured the sick
With just a word and tender hands

But He was hung upon a cross
Between two thieves He died
God's salvation for you and me
Hung tortured and crucified.

He was buried in a borrowed tomb
Lain there, He could not stay
He rose up early that Sunday morning
And Angels rolled the stone away.

Now, Jesus promised to come back
For the Church is His bride
Look up our Lord is coming soon
Hallelujah
On Heavenly clouds he will arrive.

Walking on
the Water

June 8, 1998

Jesus and Peter walked on the water one night
Everything was fine until Peter took fright.
His faith began to waiver as he lost sight
of Jesus, his Saviour, that stormy night.

Now some of us are like Peter
We start out brave and bold
But we get scared as W2-look around
We start to doubt the Saviour's hold.

Jesus held out his hand to Peter that night
And He's holding out his hands to us today
Don't do as Peter did, don't look around
for goodness sakes, don't look away.

Though Peter's faith wavered
The Lord reach for his hand
He kept the sinner from sinking
For Jesus always follows the Father's plan.

When we take our eyes off of Jesus
When we listen to the world and its din
We look inside and get defeated
because we have no power to ward off sin.

So we must keep our eyes fixed on Jesus
No matter what trouble we are in
For He will fight all of our battles
With him as our defender we can't but win.

Jehovah-Jireh

God will provide
Sometimes his provision is a place to hide.
God will provide
Sometimes his provision are the tears we cry.
God did provide
When He sent us his Son on earth to die.
God still provides
His Holy Spirit was left to be our companion, our guide.

Be it Lamb or ram when we are tried
The Lord God Almighty for us, does provide.
Gen. 22: 12-14

What a Friend

God is a friend of mine
I can talk to him anytime
I can call when I'm sad or glad
He loves it when I call him "Dad"

Jesus is a friend divine
He's my anchor in the stormiest of times
When tired and I'm sick, he heals my spirit quick
Jesus is an eternal loving friend of mine.

Jesus is my Heavenly Father's son
When In trouble to his throne I run
When I call on his precious name
He answers without scolding or blame.

Yes, Jesus is a friend of mine
He gives what I need through time
His favor doesn't cost me a dime
Jesus is my friend, He's holy and divine.

Only Dust Apart From His Spirit

His love redeemed me
His love changed my heart, my mind
His love seeks to guide me
His love is my daily sunshine

I can not live unto myself
I can not keep my soul
I can not forget God's mercy
I can not leave Salvation's fold

Lord keep me looking up
Lord keep me on my knees
Lord keep my faith steadfast
Lord keep my soul, please

Forever God was
and forever God is
Forever I am saved
Forever I am His.

Thank you Father
Thank you Saviour Son
Thank you Holy Spirit
for all the work that you have done.

It's Not Yours

Malachi 2: 10

The first fruits of all our increase, belongs to the Lord
Blessings will follow when we don't forget his commands
When we honor his name and He opens His hands.

Everything we have or are, was given to us
His grace and mercy are His unmerited favors
And His faithfulness towards us never waivers.

We must give back to the Lord what belongs to him
And don't forget to bring also gifts of love
And be sheltered by almighty hands
from our Father above.

He has promised prosperity, He keeps his word
It's His pleasure to increase us in every way
He only requires us to generously love and obey.

What does God See?

When God looks down upon mankind
Does He see the faces of anger, suffering and shame
the faces of rebellion and knowing each by name?

When God looks down into this world
Does He see the faces of sorrow, discontent and pain
the faces of pride, mourning, knowing each by name?

In our pride we attempt to ignore our pain
Being the mirrors of the soul, our eyes can't be masked,
seek healing from the Master and in His mercy, bask.
Then ...
He'll see happy people, living life rejoicingly
And when God looks down upon mankind
He'll see peace upon our faces, a
look that is holy and divine.

Ps 33: 13-15

When You are Called To Serve

God calls some to mentoring
Requiring most times self-sacrifice
There have been times when mentors
have given their very lives.

May we always remember, no matter the call
That God's mercy and grace remain true
And the power of His Holy Spirit
will triumphantly see us through.

And when ever we do for others
We will always rewarded be
All we do, have done or have given
God has afore time, ordained our destiny

Now our Lord, He is more than mentor
He is God himself ... The Christ
He did not run away nor seek to hide
He willingly sacrificed His life.

Determined Love

Sometimes I sit and wonder
At the mercy gifted to me
I look back on this life of mine
The Holy Spirit and I do agree.

I've received unmerited favor
From a Holy God on High
For nothing can I take credit
To do so would be a horrendous lie.

He's majestic, holy and tender
Caring for His creation such as we
He provided for our eternal Salvation
when His Son languished on Calvary.

But this God who turned His back
On Christ His only begotten, Son
Let Him die in painful agony
so the world through Him might be won.

Our lives are not our own you see
Christ paid a dear and awful price
So that I and hosts of other folk
would praise Him for everlasting life.

Let us praise our God, who for sinners
He willingly allowed His Son to be crucified
His grace and mercy equal purest love
And one day we will meet Him in the skies.

No Longer the Same

Our Creator, God the Saviour
Wants us to listen to His voice alone
So that He may rightly guide us
through this world unto His throne.

Scripture tells us, we are no longer
Enslaved by the power of sin and shame
He has called us out of darkness
We've been given new and holy names.

We are righteous and we are forgiven
God has claimed us for His very own
We have no time to be looking back
Children of the King, we're on our way Home.

We've been changed by His Word
Our strength is in His endless Power
His Holy Spirit now continually leads us
And in His mercy we are daily showered.

Do Everything in Him

In the Lord,
I'm believing
In the Lord
I am receiving.
In the Lord
I am so grateful
because He is
so faithful.
In the Lord
I am hoping
Because of Him
I am coping.
In the Lord
I am standing
Because I've learned
To stop demanding.
In the Lord
I am being strong
I know my Saviour
Won't lead me wrong.
In the Lord
I rejoice
Because my Jesus
Made me his choice.
In the Lord
I can testify
My hungry soul

He satisfies.
That's why I belong to Jesus
He is my Lord and my King
He is all that I will ever need
He is and possesses everything.

The Lord is Faithful

Sometimes my life seems to be drowning in hardships
my soul is crying before tears flow from my eyes
But I won't let these troubles hold me down
My Lord is in control and His love satisfies.

When I am struggling just to hold on
'cause winds of adversity blow with such force
I know that the devil is doing his best
to frustrate me and knock me off my course.

Sometimes the battle is so tiring, Lord
My will wanes as it fights to presses on
I get overwhelmed when I fail to succeed
Yet, your Word reminds, that in you I am strong

So again dear Lord, I confess my faults
And lay my troubles and failures at thy feet
Help me up again that I may walk in the Way
My desire is to overcome self and defeat.

Chapter III

*Just a Verse or Two
Saying a lot in a
Few Words*

Choose Ye This Day

Satan the opponent desires to possess you
He wants to "sift you as Wheat"
But God desires to save your soul
from the torments of Hell and defeat.

Be thou of good courage
For faithful is our King
His joy is refreshing
His love, an eternal spring.

Be Ready

God uses those who are humble
To carry out his will
So if you desire to serve him
Your will you must kill.

Beginning Again

Looking forward
I'm pressing on
All's been forgiven
I've been restored, reborn.
Given another chance, I've
Got a new song, a Holy dance
I'm happy again in Jesus
No desire for a backward glance.

Broken Hearted

When the heart breaks
Pain escapes, into the body and the mind
Love's cavity
Acknowledges hurt's depravity
As one suffers and declines.
Revive oh Lord my soul
By thy loving mercy make me again whole.

Bits of Wisdom

1.

Child of God, though your body may not be well
Your soul will not experience Hell.

2.'

No matter what you think of me
Your thoughts do not affect my destiny.

3.

Pretty is as Pretty was.

4.

If you think this kitchen is hot, to Hell, go thou not.

5.

His Spirit inspired me to pray for peace
I thought of you and my praying has not ceased.

Advice

Anger in and of itself may not be a sin
But how you handle the matter may do you in.
The Word says "vengeance is mine, I will repay"
Leave it to Him he knows the best way.

That Earthly Goal

If you don't see it
In the eye of your mind
You won't get to see it,
in the flesh of time.

If commitment is not of the heart
You won't fight for it in your soul
Your dream won't be manifested
If it is not of the spirit, foretold.

Spring

Trees are budding
Birds chirp in song
Flowers are blossoming
Summer will not be long.

Truth

Tides will recede
Fires will go out
Winds will cease to blow
Snow will melt
Tears will stop flowing
Hearts will heal
Greed will be abolished
Hatred will be turned to love
The blind will see
The lame will be made whole.

I discovered there was so much I did not know
I am appalled that my lack of knowledge is status quo.
I find there is so much I do not know
And I wonder just how it is that I still grow.

I'm Listening

When you call me
May I answer in reverent fear
Fix my heart, dear Lord
to have a listening ear.
May I recognize the sound of thy voice
Instantaneous to heed thy call
For you are my Lord and only Saviour
May your Holy Spirit ever enthrall.

Rendered Praise

O thou faithful steward
Thou all worthy of acclaim
Faithful in thy duties
Trustworthy, without blame
We thank you for dedicated service
For time, energy and talent spent
May you always exhibit His love
Always be care filled and never relent.

Room for Solitude

Sometimes l need a quiet place
So I won't think of the worries in my mind
No thoughts of when or what or how to do
Just a space, a little time ... to mentally unwind

Salvation

What a conception
What a birth
What a baby
Came to earth.
What a child
What a man
What a Saviour
My God .... what a plan!

Praise Him

Put a pep in your steps
And a smile on your face
You're alive my friend
Thanks to God's
Amazing Grace.

O Sailor

There's danger in sailing the sea of life without Jesus
So invite him on board before you set sail
And when the seas of temptations try to drown you
Jesus, Your Ark against the tempest will prevail.

Move On

You can not linger in your past
If you want to grow and live on
God is alive and ever present with mercy
Night is past
welcome and enjoy each dawn.

Love

When we ponder the love of God
And live according to his will
In those times of fault and failure
It's comforting to know He loves us still!

It's called Amazing Grace

Look Up

Keep your ears to the wind
(watch which way the trees bend)
Keep your eyes on God's Son
(it is He who for us victory, won)
And when all sorrow passes o'er
(glory will open Heaven's door)
And we'll rejoice, we'll have overcome
(our eternal Yictory, received and done.)

Look Up 'til
Jesus
Comes

I Depend on You, Lord

Lord, suffer your mercy to reign
It is your power that sustains.
Without your grace we can't hold on
Without your faithfulness there is no dawn.

I'm Sure

Standing on His promises
Jesus is the track that won't run out
So I cannot be derailed
As a child of God, I have clout.

I Belong to God

Satan, don't you touch me
I am God's property.

Formed in my Mother's womb
I was created to be free.

Jesus died for me, can't you see
I am God's property.

So, Satan you can't touch me
I belong to almighty God, I'm His Property.

Seek And Ye
Shall Find

Open up a good book
Take a real good look
Find yourself a private nook
You can learn a spiritual lesson
Even from a cook book.

The Love of God

God's love is ever flowing like a river
It soars on the wings of His Spirit
It is truth, it is honest, pure and simple
Look in His Word, listen to His Spirit
His love…receive it.

Welcome, New Born

Smile God loves you
Rejoice! For evermore
You can't begin to imagine
all that God, for you, has in store.

Smile, God really loves you
His Holy Spirit will lead and guide
Jesus, now your Saviour
welcomes you with arms opened wide.

Work of Art

I'm poetry from the mouth of God
Created for and to do good works
I am a creature who's Creator
From His commitments never shirks.

Praise God I am Me!

Frustration Cries

Lord, I gotta talk to you
So much stuff is on my mind
People get on my last nerve
Push all my buttons some time
I'm worried and I'm confused
I don't know how I'm gonna pay these bills
Father, please calm my racing heart
I need a break from the stress that kills.

Thank You Lord

Thank you for today, Father
You saw me through last night
I can not foresee tomorrow
But I can and will enjoy this day's light.

Saints!

Rise up and be who you are, a new creation in Christ
A sinner saved by God's amazing grace
You're but a sojourner here, who is
Predestinated to see God face to face.

Live up to your potential, stop groveling in the dust
Stand up and step out, in The Lord God put your trust
He will lead and guide you as you submit to His way
We only have to put our trust in Him, believe and obey.

Here's another Truth

Everything we think we know
Ain't necessarily so.
Everything we want and see
Ain't necessarily good for you or me.
Everything we think we need
Must be filtered through the Christian creed.

Deliverer

For the darkest of life's nights
We have Jesus as our guiding Light
He pierces the density of sin
and gives us strength to begin again.

Thanks

As I daily praise your name
Life I've learned is not a game
Let my faith in you, new heights attain
becoming stronger and unconstrained.

You gave your life that I might live
without reservation my life to give.
Bless me Lord to live for you
And to my vows be ever true.

Never Forget

Keep the faith, skies gray or blue
And never forget, Jesus left Heaven for you
Keep faith, truth always ensue
And never forget, Jesus suffered for you
Keep the faith, strive to live true
And never, never, never forget,
Jesus died for me and for you.

Chapter IV

Encourages /
Encouragement

Be Thou Encouraged

Be thou encouraged, for you are truly blessed
Be thou encouraged, in His spirit you are being dressed
Be thou encouraged, the battle is His not yours
Please be encouraged, the Lord is opening doors
Hold on to all of His promises
Hold on to His guiding hand
Hold on, others are watching
Gird yourself and boldly stand.
When this battle is over
Don't think there won't be more
Each trial is just a strengthener
To help you win the war.
So fight on weary soldier
Victory is just over the hill
Onward and be thou encouraged
Be a conqueror, it's the Master's will.

Press On

When years of lying and deceit
Have eroded the cord of trust
Only the Jove of God in Christ
can revive this clay of dust.
When disappointment spoils hopes and dreams
We wonder at the cruelness of men
But trust in the Lord for only He
Can ever make things right again.
When anguish and pain flood the soul
When we wonder, what is life all about
How can people be so thoughtless and cruel?
Even the truth we may begin to doubt.
We must always look unto the Lord
Expecting peace and truth from Him
The Word says He'll restore what's been lost
His faithfulness is not a fleeting whim.

Keep Trusting Him

Your faith is being tested
Hold on with all your might
Your days may be darkened
Dark as the blackest night

Focus not upon your suffering
It is your faith that's being tried
Say "Come Hell or high waters"
My God I trust and won't deny.

So do not concentrate on your trials
Your pain in peace you can endure
Don't deliberate on the circumstances
What seems impossible encourages faith to score.

Nourish Your Faith

Though I cannot be beside you in your suffering
That reality really breaks my heart
By faith you're entrusted to His care
And I know we both can then endure being apart.

Rest in the knowledge that He is with you
He'll never leave you to endure life alone
As your Comforter and friend and Saviour
Fear not, only trust the One Heavenly enthroned.

You've endured many years of anguish and pain
Your bravery is shone even through your tears
Hold on, inhale, exhale trust and keep faith
He loves you, he loves you
He's heard you down through the years.

Written to and for daughter Teal Denise
while in the hospital 2008

Obedience is better than Sacrifice

What God imparts on your heart
He will speak also to your mind
Don't hesitate (think) too long
Don't waste valuable time.

Often we don't act on what we've heard
His directive unheeded; his blessings pass by
We will have missed an opportunity to be of service
To the almighty God speaks who
has spoken from on High.

Be aware and hear what the Lord is saying
It is most wise to do whatever He may ask
For the intentions alone of your heart,
are not the obedience of doing the task.

If you want to be blessed by The Master
You must be quick to respond and to do
For there is no reward for excuses or declining,
Once you know The Master has spoken to you.

Anticipation

Let's wake up each day with a shout
Proclaiming the Word of God to be true
Look up and live the day in joy
Jesus is coming back for you.

Time is yet just a little while
Soon there'll be no need of clocks
For when Jesus does come back
The doors of Eternity will be unlocked.

Then our lives will be everlasting
And our joy will never ever end
Darkness will be a scene of the past
On God's promises we can depend.

He's prepared for His saints lavish homes
The likes of which we've never seen
Now, we can only try to imagine,
How Heaven on Earth will be like a dream.

Let's Live
His Love

We must show compassion
Denounce unholy pride
Help to comfort those in trouble
Put all prejudices aside.
We must praise Him
Though we may not understand
We must give Him glory and honor
Though we cannot see His hands.
If we are truly believers
We will strive to live holy lives
We will live as if the Angels just announced
"Today Jesus will arrive."

"Vengeance is Mine"

Let it go
Give it up
Put it down
Lift your cup.
Close your eyes
Raise your hands
Move on in peace
It's God's command.
Forgive them all
Forget their deeds
Though hard the task
Stamp out the weeds.
Don't allow anger to grow or fester
Let the Holy Spirit daily cleanse your heart
Bitterness will destroy you from the inside
Ask Jesus each day for a fresh new start.

Pray for the enemies of dissentions
Their weapons formed to destroy will fail
Keep thy head and rise above it all
Sin shall not, cannot and will never prevail.

Romans 12:19

We Must Fight to Win the Prize

In this life there are battles in this war
To be fought each and every day
Only after victory in each battle
Are we fit for the one on the way.

It's so tiring, all these skirmishes, Lord
Grant me grace to stay fit and alive
Though I know I must keep fighting,
I must run the race to get the prize.

I seek to be prepared for the battles Lord?
In thy strength each must be won
I must lift up the blood stained banner
Listening for the words, "Well done."

Make me fit for the battles, dear Lord
I don't want my striving to be in vain
I can't afford to miss the mark
Can't afford to miss that Glory train.

So I'll fight on that I may see my Saviour God
Though I'm so weary, worn and frail
I'm longing to behold my Saviour's face
I will not quit ... by faith I shall not fail.

Accept The Challenge

Be thou encouraged,
You who have climbed mountains before
Don't now, become discouraged
This one is just one more.

By continued faith and trust in God
You have scaled many hills of woe
having swam the seas of turmoil
Gird thyself again
climbing is the way to grow.

Isaiah 40:31

Bible Truth

We are not defined in God's eyes by what we do
But who we are in Him
God is not ashamed of us even when
we behave shamelessly
We can grieve the Holy Spirit of God (Eph. 4: 30)
We are His Creation, He loves us and
enables us to become his Children.

By Faith

As I walk through this day
No time to get on my knees and pray
I move through each room thanking God
For the Holy Spirit's guidance on my way.
I'm coming and going in faith and trust
Depending on God to guide this enlivened dust
I'm serving my Lord, loving him as I must
And by faith I'm living, knowing God is Just.

I am so Proud of You

I am so proud of you
In spite of every tribulation
you have stood with firm determination
I rejoice with you in sanctified jubilation.

I am so proud of you
Though you've had trials and sorrows a plenty
You have managed in faith to reverently
With thanksgiving, praise Him intently.

Enduring the trials, believing that healing will
come eventually. I am so proud of you
Keep praying as others too, beseech God for you
For He is faithful, He is kind and He is true
He has not and will not desert ... healing will ensue.
Look up His sufficient grace is enough for you.

Written for Teal Denise

What are YOU Doing?

Are you busy as a bee
in the service of the Lord
is your prayer life live and living
are you spreading love abroad?
Like the ant, be ever industrious
As you spread the Word of God
Do not rest until the seeds of truth
are planted in fertile sod.
The Lord will do the watering
Through his Spirit it will root and grow
It will flower unto salvation
For His cleansing blood did flow.
As a lion for the Master
Wield the Sword He left behind
Use it against Satan and his demons
While you sow God's love Devine.
As busy as the worker bees
As determined as the ants
And like the regal lions
Spread the Word as you advance.
Do not cease but increase the sowing
Until the Master calls to you
And you leave this world to others
Your part on earth then through
Rest assured He has others, who will carry on
They will spread the Word as you do
Never fear the sowing ended

God's got thousands more like you
When the rest of this earth's sowers
Have been born to live and die
Then know the Reaper of the harvest
will descend in glory from on High.

His command

Come
He's calling
Run
Stop stalling.
Pray
Believing
Call on Him
He'll answer
Crying?
He dries tears.
Seek
You'll find
Knock
His response "welcome" Serve
In his name
Rest
In his promises
Live
Free of guilt and shame.

Listen and Obey

What God speaks to your mind
He will lay on your heart
Don't hesitate to act
To ponder or delay isn't smart.

So, hear what He is saying
Do as the Master commands
The intent of your heart
Only counts when you follow His plans.

To reap. any blessing
You must hear, listen and do
For there's no joy in declining
when the Master has spoken to you.

An Adage of Old

Little pitchers have big ears
That is still a truth today
When in the company of any children
You'd best be careful what you do and say
In innocence they will tell on you
Repeat every word you've said
The very one you talked about
Will want to go upside your head
So be mindful of who's in your midst
Especially if your words are not meant for the world
You just may be embarrassed to the gills
When your words are repeated by a little boy or girl.

Proverbs 13:3

Keep Climbing

No matter what you hear today
Regardless to what you see
Refuse to be discouraged
Because God loves you and me.
He'll provide direction for you
His instructions are written down
His Spirit is faithfully present
Resist despair, God's mercy abounds.

We Are Set Apart, Sanctified

Anointed with the oil of faith
Healed by his sovereign will
Upheld by his loving mercy

Praise Him we're living still.
Praise God for his anointing
Pass along his Holy Word
His Spirit is alive within us
With love and power He doth gird.

Examine Yourself

Examine every one of your motives
What spirit is speaking to your heart?
Your actions scripturally based in love?
Is your service an active spiritual art?

Are you living to serve The Lord?
Do you lovingly His mercy impart?
Are you working and giving of yourself
Or just playing a scripted part?

Are you sure you are doing His will?
Are you motivated by the Master's plan?
Be sure the spirit you hear speaks true
And you serve because Love commands.

II Corinthians 13:5
II Peter 1:10-11

Nearer My God to Thee

Lord, my eyes are clouding
And my steps have begun to falter
I'm not as functional as I use to be
But thank God, I'm still your daughter.

Lord, I'm tired most of the time
Can't walk as far as I did then
Feeble in my thoughts and speech
But Lord, I remember "when".

My eyes were bright and keen
My steps were sure and strong
I remember speaking up with power
in my day, past and almost gone.

Now I'm wearing see through glasses
My choppers and grinders aren't all mine
I use a cane sometimes to support my steps
But my heart still toward Thee is inclined.

For only you have been faithful to me
No matter how I've worried or fared
I've never doubted your sovereignty
or that for me you've always cared.

I'm Brand New

(different)

It doesn't matter what I was
Only what I am and will be
It doesn't matter what I did
Only what I'm doing since salvation set me free.

What I've said it doesn't matter now
Only what I do and say
The cursing that was once the thing
He's replaced with praise and I now pray.

There is no time for me to dwell in the past
Today, in the present I'm alive
I now see a glorious future ahead
By His leading and mercy I will arrive.

Jesus is the Lord of my righteousness
He's my Saviour, my hope and my King
My life of death is dead and over
I'm reborn and my soul ever sings.

2 Cor. 5: 17

Though I Have Many Idiosyncrasies

(Formally Color Me)

Color me quiet
Color me smooth ice
Color me quite boring
Before you do, think twice

Color me very angry
Color me cool blue
Color me conspicuous
I'm gonna pray for you.

Color me lonely
Color me sadly alone
Color me pitiful
A rock that has been honed.

Color me hungry
Color me quite full
Color me somewhat greedy
But don't color me a fool.

Color me seeking holiness
Color me a humble saint
Color me trusting in Jesus
Of this world, I aint.

So you can:

> Color me forgiven
> And color me now free
> Color me redeemed
> God has pardoned me.

Ready

I'm covered, prepared to fight
I'm adorned for life's battles
My soul is anchored in the Light

I'm donning Salvation's helmet
Beautiful is my breastplate
God's love hasn't forsaken me yet,

My hands weathered for the plow
My feet directed and shod
There is no one who can stop me now.

The Spirit shall enlighten
For my heart has been changed
I'm bound most certainly for Glory
I've been assigned a new name.

Yes, the Lord has changed my name
I'm fit for The Christian war
I've been covered in the blood
I'm not a wanderer anymore.

New Born

Child of God rejoice you' re forgiven
Restored to fellowship with your Lord
He has loved and is loving you right now
You are in accord.
Rejoice in His grace
Shout! You are free
Over you Satan has no power
Life is your destiny.

Chapter V

Seasons Seasonal Times

Respect and Freedom Emerging?

Written February 2009 when Mr. Barak
Obama was elected President of the
United States of America
President Barak Obama was reelected
to office Nov. 6, 2013

Looking back upon our yesteryears
Our hearts and minds still fill with sorrow
Through the years our people sometimes doubted
There would ever be rejoicing in our tomorrows.

But God, who is always alert and faithful
Planted faith and hope in the hearts of Blacks
Even though the sufferings and abuses of our people
We praised God on the run, with hounds at our backs.

Look up and all around you my people
Life for us ain't never been no crystal stairs
But joy is comin' in the mornin' Lord
A joy filled morning on earth, we can declare.

For a people who were told when to come and go
Where to stand, sit or speak and often
like animals penned up
We've come through arduous, tragic and hate filled times
Now, my people can't you see how God is filling our cup?

Through all the struggles, toils and tears
We've been guided and lead from a mighty long way
'cause we have never been forsaken by our Maker
All those yester ways have brought
us through and to this day.

Because of His boundless grace and
mercy our souls can rejoice
He keeps his promises even in America,
the land of the free and the brave
Our God has raised us out of the ashes of ignominy and
America can no entertain treating us
as worthless, ignorant slaves.

Shout, shout, hallelujah, The Truth is marching on
No one can depreciate the value of any people forever
The worth of all mankind cannot be rightly denied
And by the Will of our God, via the majority's vote
The White House's front doors did open
Through which Mr. President Barak Obama did stride.

By the grace of God, divine ordination,
our future is more promising
And as we continue to pray in faith
believing love will increase
Pray for the World to denounce the
sin of pride and prejudice
We shall over come ... death to that beast.

Easter's Reflection Prayer

Lord, this Easter season
Remind us to worship as we look up
Let us recall why you shed your blood
Why you drank from that bitter cup.

Lord, remind us of your agony
How you endured the shame and ridicule
Just for sinners here on earth
inflicted by the unrighteous and the cruel.

Lord, remind us to look inward too
For we need revival in our souls
May we walk always in your footsteps
we're the reason for you suffering foretold.

Then Lord, remind us to look up again
To seek and by faith to behold your face
As it glows always in love on your creation
As you sit beside the Father; S, full of grace.

O' Lord, as we are looking in and looking up
And with grateful hands we give Thee praise
Let our hearts be purely filled with your love
as we live to serve Thee, all our appointed days.

Our Flag of Representation

Red denotes the color of our shed blood
Shed by many of freedom's daughters and sons
The many shades of Black is the color of our skin
So often darkened by the rays of the sky's sun
Green is the color to signify impending growth
Death will never be victor, Life is the One.

Our flag represents our determination, in God to trust
Our souls survived through bravery, sweat and tears
Our skins boldly identify us in this
world that's not our home
We could not be worked out of existence
in spite of their unjustified fears.

Red Black Green

To Mothers

Qn Mother's Da)1 we're reminded
To sing praises to our Moms
For they deserve our accolades
Like in the sacred Psalms.

Mothers are precious gifts from God
Having peace and comfort to bestow
He knows children need tender care,
By the spirit of faith, she nurtures them to grow.

Mothers can do unbelievable things
They are faithful, loving and kind
Always giving of themselves beyond measure
Never selfishly are they inclined.

We appreciate you, Mother dearest
For all of your never-ending care
For each and every sacrifice you've made
Every tear on our behalf shed and every prayer.

Psalm 113:9 Psalm 128:3-6 Psalm 127:3

God Bless us all

Heavenly Hospitality

God has promised we'll be welcomed
On that grand and glorious day
We will walk the streets of that golden city
And we'll converse with "The Way."

He promised us redemption
Eternal life and so much more
One day like graceful eagles
Into Heaven we will soar.

He has promised us new names
Clothing pure and white to wear
Promised peace and joy for ever
Not a sorrow, not a care.

Oh what joy we will experience
When we see Jesus face to face
And the Saints that will be present
All will revel in His amazing grace.

Thanksgiving Day Prayer

I will be thankful Lord, help
Remember all that you have done for me
I will allow the spirit of thanksgiving to be free
No matter what Satan or the world fires at me.

I will be thankful that you let me rise
My heart is still beating and I see with these eyes.

I am so grateful that my mind is alert
It is thinking optimistically hopeful thoughts
Not pondering past quirks and hurts.

I thank you for the water of the Word
It washes, refreshes and with hope it does gird.
I am grateful for water for cleansing my body too
For with a clean mind and clean body
I will not offend my fellowman or you.

Dear Lord, thank you for inspiring me each day
Your Holy Spirit is leading me when and how to pray.

The light of the sky faintly mirrors the Light of my soul
There's a song in my heart, revived, I'm made whole.
I'm so thankful that I know who to see
when this world and the flesh tries to discourage me.

When I give into praise, you're only a whisper away
You're the joy of my salvation, you keep evil at bay
I am grateful as I'm strengthen to live in each new day
and certain that you'll lead and guide me all the way.

Winter's Approaching

November is windy, colorful and "cool"
It's coldly beautiful and alluring
A prelude to winter's snowy drool
As children look forward to getting out of school.

November's sun most days is high and bright
Her winds gustily and forcibly blow
Her sky is clear and inviting to one's sight
We anticipate Thanksgiving with healthy appetites.

November often donates winter's white glow
And families gather 'round crackling hearths
Glancing out their windows as cottony flakes give show
All are warm and cozy sipping hot cider feeling mellow.

November

On Those Blue Days

There are days when I just can't do it
I do not strive or even try
I let the day dissipate unto its end
I'm sad but I refuse to even cry.

There are days when so hurt and tired
I don't know what to say or do
So out my window I stare but don't see
Is this what they call feeling "blue"?

In God's time, His spirit talks to me
And He reminds my soul that He's my joy
That no matter my sorrow or stress
He restrains the Devil, who desires to destroy.

So revived, I go forth in renewed hope
Knowing that my Lord to me, never lies
He's my Saviour and friend 'til eternity ends
Continuing in faith with patience, Be prescribes.

Confident in Recession/Depression

I'm not worried I'll lose possessions
I'm confident, certain and sure
No matter what this world takes from me
I've got a home in Heaven that's secure.

I'm not worried 'cause I may lack
All I possess is of temporal fare
I have a home eternal in the New Jerusalem
My Lord has promised to greet me there.

So I'm not disturbed, Heavenly Father
I believe every promise you've spoken
Regardless to the tribulations here on Earth
I'm confident in Your Word, never broken.

Autumn's Windy Arrows

Often cool crisp breezes precede winter's snow
School bells ring and leaves cascade
from tops of trees to crowded streets below.

Children wearing sweaters, scarves and caps
Daily romp through the fallen leaves
Skipping along to school and later back home
Laughingly, all enjoy pre-winter's breeze.

Salute to Mothers

You're an awesome Mother, Mom
God has done great things in you
You remained faithful in your duties
No matter what troubles you went through.

Don't concentrate on faults or failures
Let them go, to the reminders do not cling
God through your repentance has forgiven them all
His unconditional love, gives you the right to sing.

Praise God with his help you raised your children
No matter what anyone did, says or thinks
The Lord sustained you in trials and tribulations
He brought you through the waters, you didn't sink.

Lift up laboring hands and praise Him daily
Thank Him for his faithfulness, He's been true
The Holy Spirit applauds your heart's intentions
In Motherhood He's guided, He's guiding you through.

May your children praise your efforts and bless you
as they think back on their childhood days
To the happiness you've given and all you still do
Lady, you're amazing ... God bless you!

Celebration

Celebrate in holy joy
Be jubilant and gay
Christmas is a glorious time
We celebrate His birth this day.

The reds and whites of Christmas
The greens and gold we see and wear
Remind us of God's grace and mercy
Of the Glorious life He wants us to share.

So sing the songs of Christmas
And feast on happiness, faith and hope
No matter how heartless this world appears
The promises of God enable us to cope.

So Merry Christmas to one and all
Trust His Word, have faith don't doubt
For the King of Kings is alive and well
We have our Saviour to sing and shout about.

Hallelujah

The Wearing of White

Day is dawning and it is evident to early risers that all through the previous night a silently soft symphony of miniscule molecules fell, settling on expectant Earth. Happy are the children peering out of frosted windows gleefully jumping and shouting. They happily anticipate the sheer fun of sledding and snow balling and very likely "no school today" announcement.

It's the first snow fall of the season. Of course most of the adult population isn't quite as elated. They have to shovel sidewalks and clean off their cars, scrape the ice off the windshields, and put salt or sand or dirt under their car's wheels.

A noiseless gray sky speaks of winter's cold approach and the frigidness of the days ahead is evident. Get out the scarves, boots, hats and don't forget the long underwear, gloves and mittens too.

Winter will wear her cottony over coat proudly because she knows she will not have it for long. She's pleased by the laughter of the young and those still young at heart .... however brief her stay she has a purpose and a destiny yearly to fulfill. Her maker knows when to send her and when to send her down the over flowing drains into the depths of the soil to refurbish the harden soil with moisture for the spring time.

Lady Winter appreciates it doubly so at night when the street lights show off her glistening apparel to city and country bills and mountains like millions of icy diamonds, the temporary kind that melt away when the atmosphere warms the ground on a sunny day. Winter will make several appearances before the Earth begins to welcome spring flowers again and warm, fragrant scented showers.

So earth, enjoy the wearing of white while you can. Like most beautiful
things winter won't last very long and when it turns steamy, swelteringly, hot we'll wish for a cool or chilly breeze. Be thankful that we can't get bored with the weather it is so changeable thanks to our loving Creator.

Christ is Christmas

Listen to the bells as they ring
Chiming the Good News here and there
Into the world God sent His Saviour
For his shoulders, our weighty sins to bear.

How you say, that little baby
Sweet and lowly, meek and mild
All the sins of generations
could pay the cost of sin so vile.

This baby who would grow to be a man
To live a sinless life, be crucified and die
Would arise again to live for us
Our debt paid, He lives on High.

Holy love transcends impossibility
Righteous judgment requires sacrifice
Our Heavenly Father never faltered
thus His Son, Jesus the Christ.

Submission for Redemption

Long ago Jesus climbed a Hill to shame
The weight of our sins He bore
He sacrificed His pure and sinless life
Those were our stripes that He wore.

Glory to God, He arose from the grave
And in our hearts He alive and abides
He's conversing with His Heavenly Father
Look up, majestically glorious, He will arrive.

Chapter VI

Greif-Sorrow,
Saying Farewell

Sorrow will soon end

There are times when sorrow is a pit
We keep sinking deeper into
All will to fight wanes and
We just don't know what to do.

Thoughts of times gone by, increase our pain
Life without a loved one holds no joy
Emptiness is the cargo now carried
By loneliness we are now employed.

Remind my soul, precious Lord
That You are all I need
And in and through this sorrow
In your grace and mercy I can feed.

Remind me of that reunion
That will take place one glorious day
When all the Saints will meet rejoicing
Hallelujah, "Home" we shall say!

I Corinthians 15:54–57

The Sorrow of Grief

In these hours of blinding sorrow
When your soul seems to bleed
And you can't understand why
You're deprived of what you need.

As you struggle with the anger
And your flesh can only scream
Though you can't believe it now
God knows your need and dreams.

There will come a place in time
Where, when you accept His will
You'll know He's working in your life
He'll guide you through and over this hill.

And in the morning of understanding
In the noonday of your calm
When the tears don't flow in torrents
He'll remind you of truth, He is your balm.

Your heart's suffering He may diminish
Should He not it is yet His will
For grace, His grace is sufficient
You must patient, rest and be still.

There Will be A Reunion Rejoicing

There are times when sorrow is a dark pit
We seem to sink deeper and deeper into
All will and desire to resist wanes, and
We just don't know what to do.

We think of times gone by and the pain increases
life without a loved one seems to hold no joy
Emptiness is the cargo now carried
By loneliness we are reluctantly employed.

Remind my soul quickly, precious Lord
That you are all and everything I need
That in and through this sorrow
In your grace and mercy I can feed.

Remind me of that great reunion
That will take place one glorious day
When all of the Saints will meet rejoicing
Hallelujah! We shall musically say.

Be ready It's Almost that Time

There comes a time in every life
That we begin to slow down
It's the time to rejoice and have no fear
Soon we will change from hats to crowns.

The crown of life will be eternally ours
The jewels of peace will make it shine
The gems of joy, awe and grace
will mirror the holiness of the Devine.

The race we've run for many years
We'll soon be running the last lap
So don't slow down and do not stop
Don't even take a nap.

When Jesus returns and we're caught up
Joy and happiness is all we'll know
There'll be no weariness in our thoughts
Our hearts and faces will only glow.

We Will Exchange These Earthy Houses

God's children abide in all kinds of houses
T nvited, He comes in to abide in each
He's not picky, doesn't show partiality
By his example He instructs, that we may teach.

He lives in the tall and stately houses
In the lowly and rustic ones as well
He lives in the shamefully painted ones too
And with patience, their fears He does quell.

Some of God's children abide in houses
That appear lopsided or missing a wing
Their misfortune, some think, never daunts their will
As to their loving Saviour they faithfully cling.

I've seen some houses on crutches
Lots of houses using braces and canes
From inside they shout for joy unto their King
And continue on in spite of troubles or pain.

How is the house that you reside in?
Does it often resist your obedience commands?
Can His Spirit be seen through almond shaped windows?
Or does it rail at Him and voice its selfish demands?

The outside of one's house is not paramount
For the Lord doesn't measure our worth by shape or size

His loving kindness abides and encompasses our souls
When we surrender and give Him control of our lives.

We may look on some houses with scorn
Other houses with disgust or even lust
But the righteous eyes of our Saviour God
Loves every sanctified soul made from the dust.

So don't worry 'bout your looks or your lack
Remember God knows who and what you are
His love lasts forever, He fashioned and chose you
In His eyes we are His and priceless stars.

We will live forever in new, glorious bodies
Our lives governed by joy and peace
Redeemed, heavenly health never ending
In Love that will never lessen or cease.

Look up, He's Coming!

The Lord's return will not be a secret
His descent will be on the clouds
He is coming with trump and with Angels
in the company of a Holy Crowd.

We will all behold his coming
The living and those that once died
His majesty is beyond our imaginations
Our Lord gloriously descending from on High.

His subjects expectantly await His coming
We shall run to behold His grace
For He is coming in power and glory
His kingdom on Earth to raise.

Limited time

Death can only present himself in time
He now can steal a childJ abduct a wife
Sever reunions sharply like a keenly honed knife
causing the human spirit pain and strife
youth can't defy him
the elderly can't deny him
sin daily supplies him
no one can just try him.
Mercy for this time; oh Lord is our cry
Never, never our need deny
Continue as our source and abundant supply
Daily encourage our hearts, lest our hopes die
Death we know will soon have no claim
He'll never call us again by name
There's coming an end to his timely game
And he'll only have The Deceiver to blame.

When all is said and Done

My Father knows when I grieve
He knows when I'm in pain
He knows every secret thing about me
To Him there is nothing I have to explain.

He is healing my broken heart
He eases and helps me to bear every pain
He has divulged none of my secrets
Forgiven all my sins and borne my shame.

When all is said and done
I find joy and tender love in His care
He upholds me and He comforts me
All my worries and troubles He bears.

Trust Him

Though your heart right now is breaking
And salty tears cascade your face
The lord your God is faithful to you
He'll shower you with amazing grace.

Just let His love erase the shadows of suffering
And break the chains of your heart's pain
You can face and conquer any problems
In His love you 'll smile again.

For your God is trustworthy beyond measure
He's your Saviour and friend for evermore
He's your Morning Star shining brightly
With joy your faith He will restore.

As He leads you through chilly valleys
By the flames of His everlasting love
He'll remove the weight of your burdens
He'll quiet your spirit with rest from above.

Epitaph

Oh, to be remembered
When I'm asleep and gone
That kindness was my way of life
That I lived it singing a song?

For I had a mandate from the Master
In me I trust His light did shine
My goal to disperse darkness
Was His will for me, His will, not mine.

Did I show the world His mercy?
Did I try to denounce evil and ease pain?
No matter where l found misery
I trust I brought glory to His name?

Oh, to be remembered with a smile
Not a frown or angry words of distain
Did I introduce someone to Jesus the Christ
Did I make His salvation plan plain?

Oh, to be remembered for good works
Praising him always for everything
As a servant, joyfully serving my Lord
Doing my best, did I humbly honor my King?

Freedom Everlasting

In the autumns of our lives
Preparing to meet Jesus and go home
With joyous expectations
We speak and live out our Shaloms.

Happy in our abiding faith
Overjoyed in the Saviour's plan of salvation
Willing subjects of our God and King
We live our lives in favored consecration.

Bidding farewell to troubles and woes
Looking forward to the holiness of eternal light
And the promised joy beyond measure
From these houses of clay we will take flight.

Expectation

I'm on my way to see The Master
I'm on my way through nights and days
I must keep focused on my Saviour
Only He can lead me all the way.

I'm on my way to Glory land
The Lord is coming back for me
I've been on my way to Glory
Since the hour Christ set me free.

I'm on my way to lasting freedom
I'll soon be free of pains and woes
I'll be winging it to Heaven
In my new body all aglow.

All my hopes and expectations
Will be satisfied on that day
For I shall see my Saviour
Face to face in holiness arrayed.

All my prayers have been answered
When I meet Jesus in the air
I shall see Him in all his fullness
Oh, what glory with me, He'll share.

Lord, I'm looking up to see Jesus
Lord, everyday I'm on my way
I'm getting closer to our meeting
Come Lord Jesus, come today.

Sorrow

Our darkest hours in life seem to be
When death invades our lives
The tears that wash our pain-filled faces
Strengthen us to walk on, and to survive.

Our loss we cannot dismiss
There is pain that we cannot deny
So our Heavenly Father affords us
The soul's water is the tears that we cry.

When the salty floods subside
And though tried, our faith intact remains
We bless the Lord for his grace and mercy
We continue to trust his judgment all the same.

Hope to See You Soon

I know many hearts are breaking
As you look upon my house in repose
Just remember I'm really alive
My beauty like a thorn-less rose.
The real me now knows no pain
I'm care-free and in very Good Company
Forever in Truth and Light I'll be
Your grief ..... let it not be for me.

Many years of heartache I've endured
All the suffering, agony and woe
Believe me it wasn't hard to give up
To be with Jesus ... I just had to let go.

Though often I enjoyed love and laughter
A sufficient measure of hope and peace
My decaying abode seldom gave me a break
Every sinew screamed for release.

Farewell until that glorious tomorrow
We've been promised to meet in the air
We'll not remember today or the past
No more sorrow, no parting, not a care.
Jesus
Promised
To
Meet
Us
There

Things Will Change

Hold on hold out, God loves you
And He'll be with you every step of the way
You are His and the world can't steal you away.

Fight on, using spiritual might
Trust in the Holy Spirit to give you needed light
In due season, The Lord will make all things right.

Our days of struggle and toil will end soon
Peace and joy in Eternity we will spend
And fellowship with God, our Redeemer will never end.

Oh, what a time that will be
When God our Father we shall see
And from all temptation we are forever free
Oh, what a world that will be.

Heavenly Hospitality

God has promised we'll be welcomed
On that grand and glorious day
We wilJ walk the streets of that golden city
And we'll converse with "The Way."

He promised, us redemption
Eternal life and so much more
One day like graceful eagles
Into Heaven we will soar.

He has promised us new names
Clothing pure and white to wear
Promised peace and joy for ever
Minus every sorrow, free of all care.

Oh what joy we will experience
When we see Jesus face to face
And the Saints that will be present
All will revel in His amazing grace.

Chapter VII

Today is Tomorrow's Memory

Today is Tomorrow's Memory

Celebrations with our loved ones now
Make for true and lasting future memories
These times won't and can never be forgotten
these events will be reopened by memory's keys.

Make sure to memorialize all times spent together
The time will come when someone is no longer here
But if you've shared living and time with them
They will be with you all of your life, year after year.

Don't forget, though life continues on, we may not
The time we have is too short to bicker and fight
Today our family and friends are spending time with us
But one of us may be gone before the end of this night.

Be careful what you do and say when upset or angry
What you regret having said may injure a tender soul
We all make mistakes and are sorry as we repent
Restore fellowship before the injury is set and cold.

Now our pleas for forgiveness are often varied
And just because I don't do it "the right" way
Discount not, my words or gestures because you're angry
Listen through the ears of love, and believe what I say.

For many it is not so easy to say "I'm sorry"
Life's experiences may hamper one's manner of style
But when they move in obedience to the Holy Spirit
Receive their apology without vengeance or guile.

The sentiment, "I'm sorry" can be
rendered without a word
Trust the Spirit's leading .... be gracious and live
How many times have we spoken or acted thoughtlessly
How many times does our Lord God, us, forgive?

24 Hours Together

Having spent the day with you
I'm looking forward to watching the night
We can whisper in the darkness
Make love in the silence of starlight.
We'll watch the lights as the Earth rotates
Sit moonstruck on the grassy space
We'll lustfully appreciate creation in blue
Caress each other face to face.
I'm so happy when I'm in your arms
I'm at peace as we search the sky
May we live always as one
Until the day we die.

A Prayer for Restored Health

I often watch him as he sleeps
And ask the Lord, "how long"
How long Lord before he's on his feet
Erect again and strong?"

Lord, speak to his mind I pray
Sweet words of encouragement
He needs to hear Your voice, dear Lord
He is yielded and penitent.

Raise him up to praise your Holy name
He's felt your mercy and grace
On his feet may he stand once again
In his life sin and shame have no place.

Be Careful, Be Sure

Do not yearn passionately for what you think you see
Until closer you come and know it true to be
What looks from a distance like a beautiful star
Will often disappoint you, when it's were you are.

The closer we get to what we think we desire
Our nearness will often extinguish desire's fire
What we see is not always what we will get
And will more than likely increase our pain's debt.

Sometimes a person may look so good from a distance
Getting closer, your spirit might present resistance
So while you're free, better look closer and reconsider
There's the possibility that later, you may become bitter.

Living is not Easy

When I become overwhelmed
By the awesome trials in my life
I seek to hide in His presence
to rid my soul of so much strife.

When my heart feels as if it will burst
And I'm drowning in unshed tears
I know Jesus waits with open arms
To ease my burdens, eradicate my fears.

Lord, the one I love has hurt me
I've been trodden down by the pain
Don't let me fall into the well of bitterness
Lord, inspire me, my sanity to retain.

My soul rejects the awful truth
My eyes are burning from lack of sleep
My senses rage against the torment
And my body continues convulsively weep.

Lord, walk with me through these valleys
I know this will be one day only a memory be
So right now I'm holding on to you by faith
Allow my life to be a living testimony.

Betrayed

You've given what was mine to others
Without thought of me many times
You've raped my soul of trust
Devastated, for me nQthing rhymes.

Of security and peace I've been robbed
I feel betrayed, empty, and alone
I hurt, I'm crying and trying
To find my way back home.

Home is where tranquility lives
It's full of hope and joyous expectation
And happiness permeates laughter
with a sense of worth and admiration.

Betrayed, but not left
To bear the hurt all alone
The spirit of God kept me
From turning my heart to stone.

You and I

Through time and space
Through joy and pain
In love with you
I shall remain.

Though times may change
The way that you look
You'll always be "fine"
in my heart's book.

When we travel here and there
Remember always my darling
We're a couple of love birds
an inseparable pair.

It is The Love of God

I will love you

According to God's Word
Thinking myself in your place
I will love, truly love you
as a product of His Grace.
So, I am loving you
Despite the way I sometimes feel
Yes, I'm loving you still
For God's love in me is real.

People, Changed

Today is a new beginning
A chance to move up and on
God is alive and very present
Night is past, enjoy the dawn.
Look how the Lord's mercy
Shines in the eyes of others
Who once were enemies of one another
Now, they are sanctified
sisters and brothers.

Enduring Loneliness

(Flesh talking)

I mourn the absence of Eros in my life
I miss the touch of soulful passion
the company of an intimate spirited being
the satisfaction of dual reaction.

I long for the symphony of mutual compassion
Brisk times of play each winter's first snow
The companionship of long sultry walks
ardor that made our eyes glisten and glow.

Such memories are private complications
They engage the tears that scream of loneliness
To mourn the times that once were, use to be
Only creates the fodder of continuous unrest.

It's sad to realize that in me unhappiness survives
With the realization such times again, will never be
Tell me, how does the heart, full of loneliness
ever again feel cherished and carelessly free?

I am not Just a Body

Can't you see past this body
Look, I'm here beneath the skin
I am what is real and true
I refuse to be used, denied a chance to win.

I am not flesh and blood alone
I am soul and spirit and I'm free
Look past this temporal tabernacle
And you will behold the real me.

Friends?

No matter how much I relate to you
There are a few things I can not reveal
I can't open myself as one opens a book
There's a thing or two I need to conceal.

It's my pride I guess or my shame
What would you really think of me then?
Only God in His Heaven doth know
So I can't risk losing a girlfriend.
I'm sure you've not told me all of everything
I might would gasp and say "you said what, to who?"
Old folks say "chile don't tell all yo' business"
Some revelations you might later rue.

Where Are You?

How, often when I've need you
I look around and saw you not
I ponder why you're seldom here
Why I'm left alone a lot.
I often fret and worry why
Though I know you're not the all of my life
But I deserve to be treated with respect
Why?? ... because I am your wife.
Not many years more are left to us
However, I want to spend them all with you
How can you say "I love you"
And yet not do as you promised to?

Trust in God

When lies are sold ... wbo buys them?
those who seek sympathy and attention.

When lies are believed ... who eagerly receives them?
Those whose faith is weak can be easily deceived.

When a lie is told or believed ... who is grieved?
the children who have no power of reprieve.

Like the Deceiver ... deceivers spread vindictive tales
Half-truths under the guise of being truth
The Deceiver is elated when the lies are repeated
And the innocents gag on their vile vermouth.

When deceivers are gone their lies live on
And the truth gets muffled or disbelieved
In the hearts and the minds of those lied about
Honor is near impossible in this life, to retrieve.

The Word says "forgive your enemies"
Though it is our nature to seek revenge
God who loves us gives us grace to suffer
Sovereign, it's his will how and when to avenge.

Philosophical Observation

Residual feelings
Residual pain
Residual actions
Can often explain
residual emotion.
Residual memories of
residual hatred or love
the residual sufferings
one doesn't care to explain
residual residences
each in their places of shame
spawning residual reactions
to hinder and to blame.

Like a mighty wind, dislodge these ashes from the soul.

Complexity of Emotions

I, do not the act of loving
Save by the pen and in the heart
To touch my body with emotion
on–nerves me, so I retreat and depart.

I prefer to say "I love you"
And do what I'm told that love does
You need not come too close
Past behavior has distorted what was.

That fire, now a smoldering ember
I find it so hard to revive it again
Leary of the memories that might erupt
I protect myself, though I wish not to offend.

It is a lonely way to continue living
But experience has done that to me
the longings are real, but the fear that I feel
has created a heart unwilling to again yield.

Forgive this fear in me, Lord

What We Call

Love
Is
No
Excuse
To
Endure
Mental
Emotional
Or physical
Abuse

At the End of each Day

Have you digested something along the way
Was it good food for your hungry soul?
Did you spend time in God's Word?
read some New and some of the Old?

Did you fully digest even one chapter?
And determine in your heart and mind
To do service or an act of kindness
to bring joy to another of mankind?

Did you visit a neighbor who was in distress?
Clean her house, pray with her, cook a meal?
If so, know that it made her heart so happy
You'll relish how doing good make one feel.

All the acts of kindness done in love
Will put another's soul and your own at ease
A card or visit to someone in the hospital
To calm their fears, know for sure God is pleased.

Having done your good deeds this day
All while taking care of your family too
As you fellowship with the Lord tonight
Relish His presence, He's been watching over you.
No doubt smiling too.

Ephesians 2:10

The Best Thing to Do

Prov.3:2-7

As the Lord helps you to mend those fences
And you pray for wisdom and strength
Remember the battles are His not yours
Let the Holy Spirit work in your defense.

Sometimes it's best to be still and silent
No matter what is said and done
Even when you know it's not right or true
And your senses have truly been stunned.

Trust in God by faith, to work things out
Within, pray for patience and his peace
He'll bring truth to light and then
He'll cause bitterness and strife to cease.

Chapter VIII

Prayer – Praise

Through it All

In
Every
Situation
Ordeal,
Condition
God
is enough
His love
the best stuff
trust Him
each day
with
your
whole heart
Love him,
Praise him
And
Always
Pray

Jesus Prayed for Me

God the Father loveth me
The Word declares it so
My Lord did pray for me
Eternal life He did bestow.
My Saviour prayed for me
Before my soul did live
Some thousands' years ago
My Lord his life did give.
My Jesus prayed for me
So moved I am to know
The holy love of God
He suffered, for me, to show.
I thank you Lord, my Saviour
My ransom, my King and my God
I would not have known your way
If thou this earth, you had not trod
I'm so grateful for thy Holy Spirit
He seeks to guide me day by day
He comforts me in times of stress
And leads me when I pray.

John 17:1-26

Remind Me Lord

Help me to remember, Lord
That I'm not the only one
Who needs your help or who suffers
Who's lost a husband a daughter or son.

Lord, remind me of my sisters
Who also labor long and hard for Thee
Who endure scorn and suffer shame
Who spread Your Word o'er land and see.

Lord, remind me of my brothers also
Soldiers bound by their love for Thee
Stout hearted men you've called to serve
In foreign lands on foot and bended knees.

As I lift my heart and voice to thank Thee
In joy and praise for all they've done
I beseech you to strengthen each of them
until Thy Kingdom is fully come.

These committed men and women
Telling others of your matchless grace
need our prayers and financial support
to lift you up in an undying faith

When I begin to dwell on my loss or lack
Forgive me for I'm selfishly prone
Remind me to pray for the thousands more
whose losses are equal to or more than my own.

*Afford me love enough to share
and courage enough to show I really care*

Thank You

When God's people do unselfish favors
When they walk the extra miles
And pray with those in trouble
And do it with sacred smiles

The love that's shown is appreciated
It encourages the anxious soul
So we bless the name of Jesus
And His grace and mercy we extol.

You came humbly to our rescue
In our time of greatest need
We praise God for his faithfulness
He does abundantly provide and feed.

Praise and Thanksgiving for Eternal Life

I praise God for you Jesus
You are the lover of my soul
I praise God for you, Jesus
Your blood cleansed and made me whole.

I thank you Lord, you spoke up for me
Thank you Lord Jesus, one day you spoke to me
Thank you dear Lord, you still speak to me.
My state is called "Salvation"
I am Redeemed, I am free
I bless your name for saving even me.

My Prayer for Malachi

Malachi a sweet child
Chubby and fat and brown
I prayed for him each day
Before I laid him down.

I watched him grow to crawl then walk
He ate like a little pig as God daily blessed
And he prospered and grew to love me too
I trust he'll also learn to love God, best.

I miss so much that baby boy
Growing up, he'll soon be a man
He gave joy and laughter to my days
May God lead him by his almighty hand.

Grow up strong in faith and love, Malachi
Be faithful, strong and gentle too
Rely on the Spirit's leading and learn to lead
The Lord our God has plans for you.

I am, Will Be

I am an individual
There's no one just like me
The Lord is full of surprises
I was the answer to my Mother's plea.

Yes, I was created to be me
And to be a testament to his grace
Throughout my life He's been involved
Leading, undergirding so I would His way embrace.

I'm His miracle being birthed day by day
Lead through trials and tribulations
Changed and changing, I am molded
Guide me Lord, to be your Holy Salutation.

To a Christian Lady I Know

Your life is a compliment
You're a word to the wise
Always standing up for Jesus
Never do you, his mercy compromise.

You are steady and steadfast
Constant in your daily walk
You sing and joyfully live the life
Your behavior matches your talk.

So we honor you Christian lady
You are a soldier tried and true
Your life is a compliment to Jesus
And we lovingly salute you.

Thank You Lord for Mercy and Grace

I don't want what I deserve
I can't live in death's realm.

Jesus died that I might live, I know
He is in my life, He's at the helm

Sometimes rocked by current events
And tossed about by the lightning storms

Trials of this life, He has told me to
"be of good courage" they are the norm.

Lest I Forget

No matter what today annoys me
The spirit I shall employ is joy
When ignorance stands in my way
Lord, let not your peace I betray.

If in hunger I find myself
Remind me of my abundant wealth
If I have not aught to wear
Remind me of thy loving care.

Should my offspring cause me to cry
Remind me, for them too you did die
And when my curtains are drawn to close
May I recall just why You arose.

I Praise Him

I praise God for every breath I take
I safely slept last night, this morning I'm awake.
I praised him in the kitchen and in the bathroom,
and as I walked through all the rooms.

I praise him at the table, just before I eat
I praise him for his goodness, for the shoes upon my feet.
I praise him when I leave my home, I leave it in his care
I praise him on the corner as I stand waiting there.

I praise him for my husband, my children far and near
He knows all about them, he has numbered every hair.
I praise him for the approaching bus
the passengers, a seat, the driver in whom we put our trust.

I praise him when I reach my destination
I praise him when there seems to be no provocation.
I praise him for the joy and peace praise gives
I praise him and I thank him, in me his spirit lives.

Thanks So Much

For loving such as me
For your walk to Calvary
For daily setting me free
Heavenly Father, I am in awe of Thee.

For your protection of my soul
For sustaining me as I grow old
For salvation's story still told
Heavenly Father, keep me ever in thy fold.

For joy even in sorrow
For inner peace concerning tomorrow
For life that sin cannot swallow
Heavenly father, Jesus I will follow.

Praise

Lord, I lift my hands to glorify thee
I lift my voice to praise your name
I lift my heart for thee to fill it
with grace and purpose aflame.

Your children are princesses and princes
Our crowns we'll receive some day
Because our souls have been redeemed
We shall trade in these bodies of clay.

Live In Me

Holy Spirit rise and glow in me
For there are mountains I must climb
And I can't do a thing without your guidance
Give me direction at the appointed time.

No, I can't do a thing without you for
Strength and wisdom are my needs
And I'm praying that I follow your instructions
faith and trust Satan desires to impede.

Holy Spirit, my will I surrender
Seeking to always please my King
Teach me to follow in His footsteps
Alms of worship I will bring.

We Thank God for You

We, your family of nieces and nephews
Choose to give you accolades while you live
We want you to know you've been and are cherished
For you, praise and appreciation to God, we give.

We love you for your warmth and hospitality
You always make people feel welcomed and at ease
We celebrate your enormously loving spirit
And we know by faith, that our Lord you please.

Cheerful, genuinely unselfish you are
Never hesitating to meet another's needs
Child of God we bless you this day
Grateful for the numerous souls you feed.

Written for a family member of a friend RCD

A Prayer of Empathy

At times you seem so alone and confused
As to what all has happened to you
Unable to understand or express your predicament
Your bewilderment in tears you subdue.

It breaks my heart that I can't help you,
when you can't make yourself understood
I empathized at your frustration and anger
To change things, I'd do anything if I but could.

I can and do pray for the quick return of abilities
That are now seemingly lost or impaired
I can only imagine the anguish you are feeling
when you try, but your thoughts you can't share.

For a speedy and full recovery many are praying
We trust in God to heal your body and mind
Believe that He's working in and through you
The process of your healing is in His time.

We all love you and pray for you daily
Keep faith, at the end of this tunnel is the light
God's compassion and mercy are present
And his Angels stand guard day and night.

Healing Power

Healing while you sleep
From your head to the soles of your feet
Still and quiet, a rest in peace
The Lord is working the process of release.

Still and quiet, wonders never cease
For the Lord, never slumbers or sleeps
He's moving on your behalf and for your good
In your place Jesus stood.

Patience Is A Struggle For Me

Lord, I don't know how to calmly wait
For a decision, anything or anyone
Even when my body is seemingly still
My mind is determined to beat the "gun."

It distresses me to sit still and do nothing
Stillness is against my natural, impulsive will
I know you desire patience from your children
But, lord … it's so hard for me just to "chill."

Like the blood flowing through my veins
I confess my struggle remains the same
I fmd it so exasperating to wait
And of this sin too Lord, I am ashamed.
So
Lord, if confession is good for the soul
I confess my impatience to Thee
Teach me to live in patient peace
Strengthen my resolve to on others and Thee.

Listening to Me Lord?

I'm trying to pray, Lord
Think I'm just mouthing words.

My heart is in so much pain
I'm not sure my speech is plain.

So in silence I bow before Thee
Anguished, I utter only sounds
Allow thy Holy Spirit Lord
To keep me planted on solid ground.

Give me strength for this day, oh Lord
My heart is torn seemingly in two
I'm not sure of what I'm saying
Or what it is I'm now to do.

I am sick to my soul and so weary
I can't go on, can't continue in this way
How could he, how? Again,
How could he me, betray?

Prayer

As I watch him deep in sleep
I ask the Lord, "how long,
How long before he's on his feet again
confident and strong?

Please Lord, speak to his mind
Tender words of encouragement
His spirit needs to hear your v-0ice
his heart's now yielded, it's penitent.

Raise him up to be the man
You've always intended that he should be
Fill him with your spirit of love
That he may proclaim his freedom in Thee.

A miracle we ask, oh Lord in Jesus' name
Welcome your child back home
lift him up to stand erect
having destroyed the desire to roam.

Then he can bless your Holy Name
And sing praises for the rest of his days
Oh, what a testimony be will be able to give
Of thanksgiving, your mercy and grace.

This Parent's Prayer Letting Go and Trusting God

Teach me to appreciate my children's rights, Lord
Despite their faults and mine that I see
You know that I love alJ of them, may they grow in love with thee.
Teach me to respect their adulthood
Good or bad their raising is done
I can't make or forsake them, but strive daily to show them your Son.
Remind me that it's their right to go their own ways
They are no longer accountable to me
They must answer to you and acknowledge salvation in Thee.
Help me to resist the temptation to change them
And to remember there are boundaries I must respect
They must live and learn, fall or stand in Thee, it's your joy to correct.

All my directing and my protection
Must now cease and desist because
They are no longer my little children .... they must respect and obey Your laws.

May I never show, or expose any signs of being disappointed in them
Never cause them shame or distress (though I may have, I hope they forgive me) They are blessings from your hands and I pray for their successes.

Because We Belong to You

Have Thine own way, Lord
Your children belong to Thee
So lead us and guide us
from earth to eternity.
Teach us to always have faith in you
To work all things out for us
During each trial or tribulation
Remind us, in you to keep our trust.

Intercession

When it's laid on your heart to pray
Perhaps for a special person today
Lift them high unto the Lord
And in the spirit pray in accord.

That someone may be troubled or in pain
feeling the affects of sin or shame
Though he or she may have fallen
Ask Jesus to remind them of their calling.

That someone may be grieving
Or standing in the gap for one who is leaving
Remind the Lord of His promises true
you're depending on Him to see them through.

Today is this one's intercessory time
Tomorrow another may be placed on your mind
So do all that you can in a spiritual way
lift them in prayer continuously, all through this day.

Christians Sing

We sing when we are happy
We sing when we are sad
We sing because He loves us
We sing 'cause He's our Dad.

We sing because we've been forgiven
We sing because we're free
We sing to praise our Saviour
No longer burdened by quilt are we.

We sing because He'll guide us
Over mountains, through valleys so low
We sing as we travel in faith
In this wilderness here below.

Lord, we sing because we love you
We're so grateful for your tender care
We sing because you're Holy and righteous
When we get to Heaven you will welcome us there.

Good morning Lord

I awoke to a classic daybreak
Illuminated by that heavenly sphere
I was moved to engage all my senses
I smiled as they all obediently cheered.

My eyes beheld blinding radiance
My flesh welcomed its rays
My nose pulsated in the scent of fresh dew
My ears pricked to the distant neighs.

I lifted my head, hands and heart
To be bathed in reverent glory
Renew my soul again today, dear Lord,
So that I may re-tell your story.

Telling it Like it Is

Misunderstood
Why is that so
I've been praying Lord
I want to change and in you to grow.

I'm misunderstood
And sometimes I don't understand
Why the thing I desire to say
doesn't come out as I planned.

When I've hurt someone unintentionally
Apologize and try to explain
My words are not always accepted
And my patience is strained.

Then I get angry,
"why would you take it that way
don't you know me by now
can't you read what I say?"

Troubled in my Spirit

I sense a call to pray
Lord, you know the reason why
my heart is troubled
I withhold the tears to cry.

Increase my courage make me to sing
for in my heart sin hides there
I confess my failure and rebellion
Holy Spirit cleanse me from despair.

I am yours Lord, You know that I am
You bought my freedom a long time ago
Though often willful and waywar, l'm yours
In this flesh I'm struggling here below.

But I expect you to keep your promises
and restore me when I fall down
and pick me up and brush me, your needy child off
I'm weak Lord, but I so desire to wear that crown.

Scripture

Turn It Over to Jesus

Lord, may I give my pain to you?
All the hurts I can not bear?
Sometimes my soul's so heavy
That tears are my way of prayer.

Lord my sins have been laid at your feet
And I bow my head confessing thou are Holy
I lift up adoring hands to praise you
You are my Saviour, and I worship you boldly.

Though I'm tired, bewildered and weary
Lord, my burdens I've just got to share
Though You are awesome and royal
I have no doubt that for me, you care.

Proverbs for Abundant Living

Listen, it's the way to learn
Working is the way to earn.

The happy heart smiles via the face
The mercies of God depict his grace.

Worry weighs even the mighty down
a painted smile but makes a clown.

HI would be a faithful saint
In service daily I must not faint.

From the core of the heart give all
Pray for those who by the wayside fall.

When in trouble pray your way through
The Holy Spirit will enable and encourage you.

A life that's balanced won't tip the scales
To the praying heart His will He unveils.

A Christian's Prayer for the Unsaved

Heavenly Father hear the cries of sinners
Relieve the souls who search for peace and rest
Let your Holy Spirit calm their faltering hearts
Show them Jesus, the Saviour who came to bless.

Holy Spirit, as they cry out in repentance
Enter and surround them in heavenly peace
Let them know the cleansing mercy of forgiveness
That they are from Satan's power free and released.

Fill their hearts with daily thanksgiving
And their minds to continually worship thee
Lord, saturate their souls with undying faith
And a love so true, that even the world can see.

Joy sorrow
Peace war
Laughter tears
Life's balance what's more.

Living dying
Life death
Singing dancing
By design by request

Sick well
Gain lose
Nothing here is for ever
Why sing the blues?

Like me love me
Hate me enslave me
A time for all things Freedom
God gave me.

May We Abide

Lord, help us through this grief and loss
Through this valley so deep and wide
And as the tears from hearts do flow
May we grieve as in Thee we abide

Remind us there is a bright tomorrow
Our tears will then be those of joy
And all pain will be forgotten
Death and sorrow destroyed.

What I Must Do?

I must learn to be compassionate
Exude mercy unto the weak
See them as the Lord sees them
Saints who are rising toward their peak.
I must show compassion
Denounce unholy pride
Aid those who are in trouble
Put all ungodly prejudices aside.
I must forgive the ones who've hurt me
Down through the years, everyone
For I long to see my Lord in peace
His commandments having been done.
I must love my enemies as I do my friends
Not just in words but in every deed
Cause I want to go to Heaven, Lord
Help me to obey my Saviour's creed.
I must walk in his footsteps
Trusting him each and every day
Love my neighbor, be a faithful servant
Read my Bible and fervently pray.
I owe my life to God the Father
For He gave Jesus up for me
I can not repay the debt I owe him
But I sure am grateful that He set my soul free.
The Bible says in Glory we will worship him forever
The One who made life possible for eternity
I can only imagine the beauty our eyes will behold
when we're no longer blinded by my, mine, and me.

I'm stuck in a rut don't know how to get out
Taking another job is out of the question
Nobody believes me when I tell them
"There ain't no more jobs, we're in a depression".

A Glimpse of Jesus

Let me tell you about my Jesus
He's my Father's only begotten Son
He came to earth a long time ago
My freedom from Hell He won.

Let me tell you about my Jesus
Born a miraculous virgin birth
Laid in a stable's manger
while Angels sang in gleeful mirth.

Great men sought to kill him
Fearful of his sovereignty
Wise men traveled just to behold him
This child, come to set men free.

Let me tell you about my Jesus
He's the Son of the living God
He's the lover of my sin sick soul
As a sinless man this earth He trod.

Let me tell you about my Jesus
Baptized by Saint John in the Jordan
Before all, The Father verified his deity
identified and glorified, He did stand.

Jesus was lead into the wilderness
Tried by the Evil One, He passed every test
Then He started on his mission, healed some sick
forgave sins and the lame did walk by request.

Let me tell you about my Jesus
For He called to me one day
Convicted of my need and my sins
I was forgiven and cleansed in every way.

He doesn't just heal broken, sick bodies
He is the power that heals sin sick souls
He's concerned about the whole person
Complete salvation is my God's goal.

Telling it Like it Is

Misunderstood
Why is that so
I've been praying Lord
I want to change and in you to grow.

I'm misunderstood
And sometimes I don't understand
Why the thing I desire to say
doesn't come out as I planned.

When I've hurt someone unintentionally
Apologize and try to explain
My words are not always accepted
And my patience is strained.

Then I get angry,
"why would you take it that way
don't you know me by now
can't you read what I say?"

Troubled in my Spirit

I sense a call to pray
Lord, you know the reason why
my heart is troubled
I withhold the tears to cry.

Increase my courage make me to sing
for in my heart sin hides there
I confess my failure and rebellion
Holy Spirit cleanse me from despair.

I am yours Lord, You know that I am
You bought my freedom a long time ago
Though often willful and wayward I'm yours
In this flesh I'm struggling here below.

But I expect you to keep your promises
To pick me up if I should fall down
and restore your wayward child
Lord, I so desire to wear that crown.

Turn It Over to Jesus

Lord, may I give my pain to you?
All the hurts I can not bear?
Sometimes my soul's so heavy
That tears are my way of prayer.

Lord my sins have been laid at your feet
And I bow my head confessing thou are Holy
I lift up adoring hands to praise you
You are my Saviour, and I worship you boldly.

Though I'm tired, bewildered and weary
Lord, my burdens I've just got to share
Though You are awesome and royal
I have no doubt that for me, you care.

Proverbs for Abundant Living

Listen, it's the way to learn
Working is the way to earn.

The happy heart smiles via the face
The mercies of God depict his grace.

Worry weighs even the mighty down
a painted smile but makes a clown.

If I would be a faithful saint
In service daily I must not faint.

From the core of the heart give all
Pray for those who by the wayside fall.

When in trouble pray your way through
The Holy Spirit will enable and encourage you.

A life that's balanced won't tip the scales
To the praying heart His will He unveils.

A Christian's Prayer for the Unsaved

Heavenly Father hear the cries of sinners
Relieve the souls who search for peace and rest
Let your Holy Spirit calm their faltering hearts
Show them Jesus, the Saviour who came to bless.

Holy Spirit, as they cry out in repentance
Enter and surround them in heavenly peace
Let them know the cleansing mercy of forgiveness
That they are from Satan's power free and released.

Fill their hearts with daily thanksgiving
And their minds to continually worship thee
Lord, saturate their souls with undying faith
And a love so true, that even the world can see.

May We Abide

Lord, help us through this grief and loss
Through this valley so deep and wide
And as the tears from hearts do flow
May we grieve as in Thee we abide

Remind us there is a bright tomorrow
Our tears will then be those of joy
And all pain will be forgotten
Death and sorrow destroyed.

What I Must Do

I must learn to be compassionate
Exude mercy unto the weak
See them as the Lord sees them
Saints who are rising toward their peak.

I must show compassion
Denounce unholy pride
Aid those who are in trouble
Put all ungodly prejudices aside.

I must forgive the ones who've hurt me
Down through the years, everyone
For I long to see my Lord in peace
His commandments having been done.

I must love my enemies as I do my friends
Not just in words but in every deed
Cause I want to go to Heaven, Lord
Help me to obey my Saviour's creed.

I must walk in his footsteps
Trusting him each and every day
Love my neighbor, be a faithful servant
Read my Bible and fervently pray.

I owe my life to God the Father
For He gave Jesus up for me
I can not repay the debt I owe him
But I sure am grateful that He set my soul free.

The Bible says in Glory we will worship him forever
The One who made life possible for eternity
I can only imagine the beauty our eyes will behold
when we're no longer blinded by my, mine, and me.

Printed in the United States
By Bookmasters